SAFE ROADS MAKE A HAPPY CITY

RULES OF THE ROAD

USE A SEATBELT   OBEY TRAFFIC SIGNALS   DON'T DRINK AND DRIVE   WEAR A HELMET   FOLLOW LANE DISCIPLINE

Initiated By
SAB MILLER | India

FOLLOW THE RTR TROUPE
 @respecttheroad

JOIN THE CONVERSATION
 Facebook.com/respecttheroad

Experience divinity with a touch of gold.

The Golden Temple in Amritsar has never failed to strike awe and tranquility into even the hardiest of unbelievers. Built in 1574 AD, this gleaming shrine is a sight to behold. But there's more for the divinity seekers. Visit the Durgiana Mandir, Guru-Ka-Mahal, Pipli Sahib and the Akal Takht. If you want a different point of view, visit the Wagah Border, Jallianwala Bagh, Ram Bagh and Harike-Pattan wetlands. All these, a stone's throw from the Golden Temple. So, come to Punjab and go on a spiritual journey unlike any.

www.punjabtourism.gov.in

PERHAPS YOU SHOULD VISIT THE PLACES YOU SEE IN THIS BOOK.

Explore Karnataka. Begin your journey from
Kempegowda International Airport, Bengaluru.

YOUR JOURNEY STARTS FROM HERE...

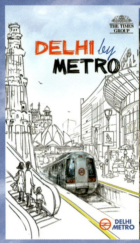

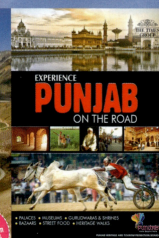

To order your personal copy please log on to www.amazon.in, www.flipkart.com and www.infibeam.com or write to us at tgb@timesgroup.in.
Available at all leading bookstores.

MORE THAN JUST AN AIRPORT, A DESTINATION

Bengaluru, the Silicon Valley of India today defines the country on the global arena. Few Cities in the World have the power to attract and motivate a visitor with its vibrancy and rhythms of the unfolding future. Bengaluru is one of those rare cities that create a lasting impact as a vivacious young city.

Bengaluru is in a class of its own when it comes to redefining flamboyance. Bengaluru has attracted a lion share of well-educated migrants from across India and is seen as the Capital of New Age Industries and Sunshine businesses: IT, ITES, Bio-technology, aerospace and others. This city has increasingly gained the tag of the startup capital of India as well.

No surprise then, Kempegowda International Airport, Bengaluru (KIAB) today is the 3rd largest domestic aviation market. It is also the busiest airport in South India. Being a major hub for passengers flying into South India, KIAB offers a welcoming glimpse into the state's cultural and historical heritage. KIAB understand its role in the promotion on tourism. Combining unparalleled growth prospects and unlimited potential, KIAB is on the foyer towards being a key player in the changing face of the regions tourism. More than just an airport, a destination.

EXPERIENCE
KARNATAKA
ON THE ROAD

EXPERIENCE
KARNATAKA
ON THE ROAD

SUPRIYA SEHGAL

First published in India, 2016

 **A division of
Bennett, Coleman & Co. Ltd.**
The Times of India, 10 Daryaganj, New Delhi-110002
Phone: 011-39843333, Email: tgb@timesgroup.in

EXPERIENCE KARNATAKA: ON THE ROAD

Copyright ©Bennett, Coleman & Co. Ltd., 2016

All rights reserved. No part of this work may be reproduced or used in any form or by any means (graphic, electronic, mechanical, photocopying, recording, tape, web distribution, information storage and retrieval systems or otherwise) without prior written permission of the publisher.

Disclaimer
Due care and diligence has been taken while printing and editing the Book. The Publisher does not hold any responsibility for any mistake that may have crept in inadvertently. Tariffs may have changed from the time of publication.

Photographs: Supriya Sehgal, with contributions from Abhishek Das Gupta, Malabika Ghosh Das, Jaita Mullick

ISBN: 978-93-84038-29-8

Price: ₹349

Printed at: Lustra Print Process Pvt. Ltd.

CONTENTS

SAVOURING THE DIVERSE...14

DRIVING ROUTES & HIGHWAYS...20

GETTING ACQUAINTED WITH KARNATAKA...34

BENGALURU...50
    Day Trips from Bengaluru...74

MYSURU...84

THE HOYSALA TRAIL...98
    Bengaluru ▶▷ Hassan ▶▷ Belur ▶▷ Halebeedu

THE COASTAL ROUTE...110
    Mangaluru ▶▷ Udipi ▶▷ Jog Falls ▶▷ Gokarna ▶▷ Karwar

GORGEOUS GREEN...144
    Bandipur ▶▷ Kabini ▶▷ Kodagu

COFFEE & TREKS...160
    Hassan ▶▷ Chikmagalur

SYLVAN TRACK...172
    Shimoga ▶▷ Hubli/Dharwad ▶▷ Dandeli

HISTORY UNRAVELLED...184
    Badami ▶▷ Pattadakal ▶▷ Aihole ▶▷ Hampi

STORIES IN STONE...206
    Vijayapura ▶▷ Bidar

TEMPLE TRAIL FOR THE SPIRITUALLY INCLINED...216

FOOD OF KARNATAKA ON A MAP...218

INDEX...222

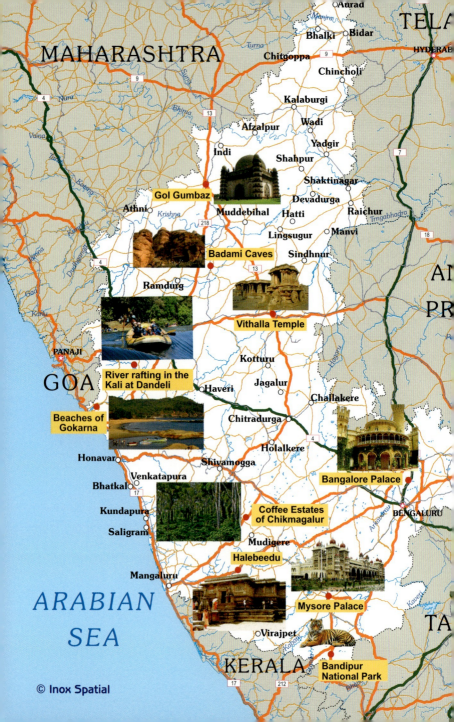

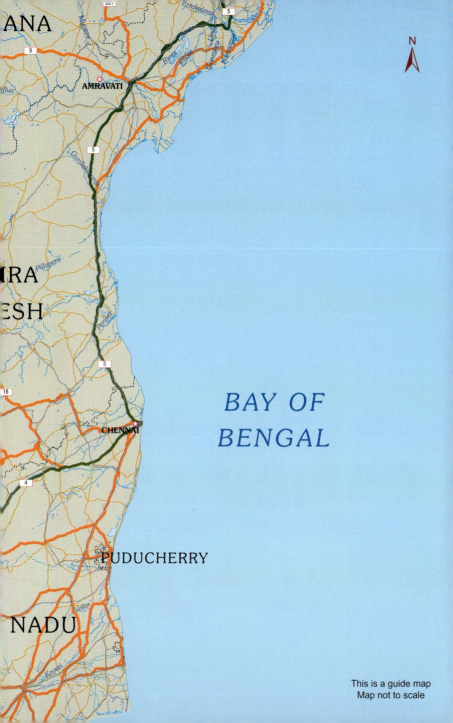

Savouring the Diverse

For the last decade, the culture of self-driving holidays has taken over top Indian cities. While one could attribute it to a sense of adventure, fun, flexibility or freedom, it definitely makes a rewarding choice as compared to booking tickets on trains and buses. Moreover, tourists can pace the journey according to their preference. Besides, well-constructed, motorable roads and necessary amenities such as hotels, restaurants & eateries and petrol/diesel pumps have popularized road travel across parts of the country. Amongst these, in southern India, Bengaluru (earlier called Bangalore), the capital city of Karnataka, holds a veritable position, as this state itself presents some of the most diverse and easily accessible destinations of interest. Not only do several destinations in Karnataka lend themselves perfectly to this nature of travel, but the infrastructure in highways, pit stops, sightseeing interests on the way and an inclination towards adventure synthesize to make the state rife with self-driving options. A network of national and state highways spans across Karnataka to facilitate access. Sandwiched between the Arabian Sea and the states of Goa, Andhra Pradesh, Kerala, Tamil Nadu and Maharashtra, these drives often spill onto the neighbouring states.

Karnataka's easy-to-navigate roads will connect you to a wide array of holidaying ideas. From awe-inspiring landscapes to ancient temples and wildlife haunts, the state is brimming with experiences. Other touristy places include beaches, coffee plantations, spiritual hooks, dense forests, tea plantations and outdoor themes. You will find unique destinations not more than 350km away from any one nodal city of Karnataka like Bengaluru, Hubli, Mangaluru (earlier Mangalore), Hampi, etc., and it is easy to club a variety of experiences within these. In fact, some of the major destinations lie on the routes radiating from Bengaluru. Others, in the northern part of Karnataka, can be reached from other major hubs. The city of Mysuru

◀ Bejewelled: Elephants at the entrance of the majestic Mysore Palace

Experience Karnataka

(earlier Mysore) is yet another significant nodal junction as far as self-driving holidays are concerned. This travel handbook, with its focus on highways, road conditions, pit stops and suggestions for best-known attractions and accommodation – from luxurious hotels to cosy family-run guesthouses – to suit all budgets, will give you plenty of reasons to be on the road while travelling in Karnataka. While there are multiple routes to a place (as in any other state/city), with subsequent variations in distance and kilometres, the most travel-friendly routes (and kilometres) have been mentioned here.

Within the destinations, you will find several themes that bind a trip together or a single trip can also have nuances of many travel propositions. Some of the themes that are apparent in the guide are mentioned below.

ALONG THE COAST

The Karnataka coast stretches along the edge of the Arabian Sea, making it one of the top routes to explore. The drive is dotted with historical points of interest and a vivid landscape that is hard to not get curious about. Veer off into villages, temple towns and even try your hand at the many adventure-sport activities that have popped up here in the last few years. One of the most unexplored but exciting routes in Karnataka, the coastal journey is fast becoming popular.

NATURE AND OUTDOORS

There is no dearth of destinations in this state that clubs together the excitement of camping in the woods, trekking trails and the great wide open.

Verdant Karnataka: A treat for urban eyes

Ideal wildlife destination: Wildlife sanctuaries of Karnataka, part of the Western Ghats and the South Vindhyan mountains abound in wildlife

From Galibore, Bheemeshwari, BR Hills or even camping by the Harangi Dam, the options are aplenty. The varied topography of Karnataka presents a plethora of ideas for experiencing nature at its best. In fact, the verdant forests of Karnataka are some of the densest in the world, offering their fringes to a number of nature and outdoor enthusiasts.

WILDLIFE

An extremely popular road trip in Karnataka presents itself in the form of wildlife-specific destinations. Amplifying this is the Nilgiri Biosphere Reserve of the Western Ghats of India, which gives Karnataka an opportunity to access both tropical and sub-tropical forests that collectively make a UNESCO-considered world-heritage site. These include Bandipur, Mudumalai, Mukurthi and Wayanad reserved forests that straddle boundaries with different states. Animal sightings of Asian elephants, leopards, gaurs, wild dogs, hyenas, spotted deer and even tigers amongst

Experience Karnataka

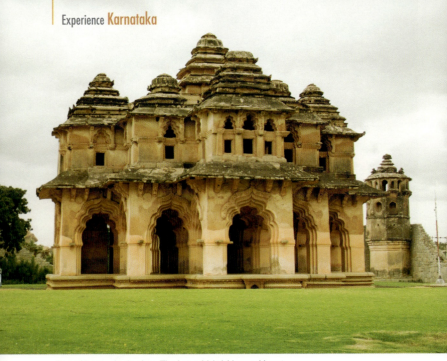

An architectural splendour: The Lotus Mahal, Hospet, Hampi

many other species are not uncommon. Flora and avian life in the region are also spectacular. These destinations have increasingly been sustained and backed by an efficient tourism industry with several eco-savvy options to stay and things to do. Bandipur, Masinagudi, Kabini or River Tern are likely to fall on your wildlife sojourn.

HERITAGE

Aged monument and architecture trails bear testimony to an impressive legacy of kingdoms from centuries ago. For history enthusiasts, these destinations transcend you to a world that was unknown. Amidst many, the legacy of the Vijayanagar kingdom (1336–1646) that impacted a large part of southern India is one of the most popular explorations. The ruins of the kingdom still make the impressive bouldery topography of Hampi and Anegundi. Likewise, the Hoysala kings' fervour for building exquisite temples is revealed in Hassan, Belur, Halebeedu and Somanathapura. Yet another section of the state that receives thousands of tourist imprints in the winter months is the area in and around Badami, Pattadakal and Aihole.

HOLISTIC HEALING

Karnataka is also home to some covert yet exceptional establishments of holistic healing. From Camilla Parker to Arvind Kejriwal, many have travelled here for healing sessions with expert practitioners. While on the road, these special spots command a few weeks on their own.

SPIRITUAL

Along with the diverse heritage of the state, there is an intense spiritual vibe that is captured in the ancient temples of the state. Of these, Sri Udipi Krishna, Mookambika, Sringeri, Gokarna, Dharamsthala, Chamunda Devi and Shravanabelagola are some of the top destinations that come en route. A stop is worth your while, to marvel at these ancient creations, some of them so timeless, that it is difficult to trace their origin.

COFFEE PLANTATIONS

It is difficult to extract the theme of coffee out of Karnataka. After all, the state is home to three of the most important coffee-producing stalwarts of India: Sakleshpur, Kodagu (earlier Coorg) and Chikmagalur. Thick with undergrowth and a million shades of green, the plantations and surrounding areas make for brilliant holiday themes, coupling the plantation life with a refreshing dose of nature. One of the most popular getaways for city dwellers, the coffee-covered hills of Karnataka are a great option when the road ends in a vintage cottage, complete with fireplace and a sprawling veranda, reminiscent of colonial architecture. This is a place to unwind.

Lush coffee plantations in Karnataka are a major attraction for tourists

Driving Routes & Highways

If you want to experience the true Karnataka, and feel the heart and soul of the state, chances are that the rendezvous on the road might be more impactful than the destinations themselves. Some of the main highways and detours are likely to add an interesting dimension to your trip. It can be a challenge to adequately sum up small unassuming *chai* shops, shanties that dish out the best dosas or scenic spots that will urge you to pause awhile to soak in the view and environs, to halt and take a break from your driving. Each season, hour and bend in the road promises new discoveries.

In this chapter, divided under sections, are some key highways, with a description of the road conditions, expected sceneries and essential pit stops.

SECTION A
Bengaluru and Mysuru
ROAD CONDITION

The Bengaluru–Mysore Road is SH17 (State Highway 17) and one of the most important exits of the city. It runs across the state for 149km, through the towns of Ramnagar, Channapatna, Maddur, Mandya and Srirangapatnam and is a double-lane highway. Expect smooth roads, interjected with busy clusters only near the cities. Be warned about traffic clogging on weekends, as many self-driving enthusiasts head out to places like Mysuru, Kodagu, Kabini, Bandipur, Masinagudi and Kerala, which can be accessed from this road.

EXPECTED SCENERY

The erstwhile countryside ambience of SH17 has been rapidly changing to that of being flanked by infrastructure and construction. Some parts on the highway do give you a glimpse of fields, low semi-deciduous forested hills and ravines broken by thin capillary-like water systems.

◄ Cautious and alert driving is necessary when travelling in and around national parks & wildlife sanctuaries

ESSENTIAL PIT STOPS

Dodda Alada Mara or the Big Banyan Tree: To get to this locally popular tourist spot, you will have to drive 28km out of the city and take a right after Kengeri on the Bengaluru–Mysore Road. At the end, almost 6.5km from here, lies a vast expanse of dropping roots for 3 acres. The 400-year-plus old tree is an awe-inspiring phenomena. There is some seating available at the park-like place but be warned that the mammoth tree is supervised by a gang of monkeys. An interesting stop, just out of the city, it certifies you as a true-blue Bangalorean if you have visited here.

Wonder La: One of India's most professionally managed amusement parks, Wonder La came up in Bangalore in 2005, just off Bidadi, 29km from the city. Spread over more than 80 acres, the park is likely to be crammed on weekends. With more than fifty water-and-land-based rides, it is a stop made in heaven for children. You could spend an entire day, stay at the in-house resort and then go ahead on the same road.

Channapatna toys: Colourful toys made from soft wood

Channapatna: The Persian art form of making wooden toys and lacquerware, which was once popularized by Tipu Sultan, can still be seen in this small town after Ramnagar. The toys are made from the soft wood of a local aale mara tree that cannot be used for furniture. The wood from the tree is cut into blocks, made moisture-free in a shed and then hand- or machine-chiselled to make toys and educational objects. These are then painted with bright vegetable (non-toxic) dyes. The finished products have found their way to countries as far as Japan. A number of shops flank the highway as one passes through Channapatna – the most prevalent toy being the wooden horse. To pick up attractive souvenirs, you can visit the Katerpillar shop at Kadambam Restaurant. Contact the owner, Mr Venkatesh on 080-27253358 in advance if you want to visit his toy-making unit.

Ramnagar: Immortalized by Bollywood as the den of the dreaded dacoit Gabbar in the 1975 blockbuster film, *Sholay*, Ramnagar still holds the appeal for many. Add to that, a scape conducive for rock climbing, a Rama temple

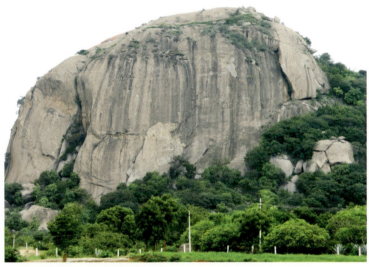

The Land of Seven Hills: Craggy and rocky Ramnagar is a must for outdoor enthusiasts

perched high on a craggy hill and endangered yellow-throated bulbul and the long-billed vulture population, this is a great pick for wildlife and outdoor enthusiasts. It arrives only 50km after driving out from Bengaluru. Ramnagar also boasts being the largest silkworm cocoon market in India.

Innovative Film City: Another stop relevant for young tourists, Innovative Film City lies 36km from Bengaluru; take a left from Billakempanahalli. The film city offers a range of adventure sports, museums, an aqua kingdom, petting zoo, food courts and more in its sprawling area.

Kamath Lokaruchi Hotel: An iconic establishment that is often packed with hungry travellers, Kamath Lokaruchi is buzzing with activity, no matter what time you enter. If you are lucky to get a table, be ready for a steady supply of authentic Kannada cuisine like Jowar Bhakri meals, Karavali (Coastal) vegetarian meals, Ragi Mudde meals, Moode Idli, Kadubu, Ragi Dosa, Neer Dosa, Akki Rotti, Maddur Vada, Otthu Shavige, Holige, Dink Laddoo, Dharwad Peda, Kashaya, sugar cane juice and more.

Kadambam: Just after Channapatna town, Kadambam Restaurant is yet another favourite breakfast haunt; the Thatte Idli (large flat pancake-like idli) finishes swiftly on holidays. The highway pit stop's popularity is evident from the parking lot itself. Even at 7.30 a.m., cars pour into the lot and fit themselves with lego-like precision. Puliyogare (tamarind rice), Thatte Idli and a cup of filter coffee are the staple favourites.

> **ALERT:** Beware of small children begging for money or pencils in lieu of showing you these birds. One really does not need any assistance or guide into the village, so it is recommended not to encourage the kids to beg.

Kokkare Bellur: A bizarre flock of painted storks and spot-billed pelicans have adopted a small village 21km off Channapatna (13km left from the highway). A number of visitors meander though the scenic village road to Kokkare Bellur to see this striking spectacle. Most of the trees and rooftops are packed with these avian friends, who do not venture outside the village limits. The villagers are used to the persistent cacophony from all around and consider their village blessed as the chosen spot for these birds. There is a small enclosure from where some of these birds can be seen in closer proximity.

Heritage Winery: Swing left, just after Channapatna and before Kadambam Hotel, 1km inside, to the Heritage Winery. A rustic backdrop to the bottling plant, an open restaurant and a small educative video on wines in India waits at the Heritage Winery. You can book ahead for a guided tour and tasting for 45 minutes to an hour. Contact Linet Sequeira, Ph: 09741798666, 10.30 a.m.–5 p.m.

Maddur: The only veritable reason for one to stop 81km from Bengaluru at Maddur would have to be to pack some Maddur Vada – a fritter-type savoury snack. A standard offering on the 'tiffin' menu, it is worth your while if you are a fan of this coconut-flavoured, dry, savoury snack. Maddur Tiffanys is where you should be heading to taste a recipe that has been doing the rounds since the last hundred years.

A priest amidst prayers and offerings to Lord Gomateshwara in Shravanabelagola

SECTION B
The Hoysala Trail (Bengaluru–Hassan–Belur–Halebeedu)
ROAD CONDITION

The Bengaluru–Hassan route is the access stretch for the Hoysala themed towns of Belur and Halebeedu, along with some of the other sightseeing interests like Shravanabelagola and Sakleshpur, which lies further ahead. The most convenient road – and a faster route – to take is NH48 (National Highway 48), which passes through Channarayapattana, the access point to Shravanabelagola, an important religious site for Jain devotees. The 185-km distance between the two cities on this highway can be covered in less than 3 hours – after the road was upgraded to a four-lane highway. This is one of the best links between the state capital and the Malnad districts along with the coastal belt. With traffic growing on this stretch, NH48 is a significant relief for travellers.

EXPECTED SCENERY
The earlier avatar of this stretch, minus the highway, was dotted with a number of countryside scenes but now the view is mostly of a long, smooth, steel-grey tolled road. Palm fringes peep from edges of the highway, offering some relief to the eyes.

ESSENTIAL PIT STOPS
The massive statue of Bahubali in Shravanabelagola is the postcard picture of the Hassan–Belur–Halebeedu circuit of Karnataka. Though the town has no connect with the Hoysala path, it is easy to club it on the same route. A Jain pilgrimage, Shravanabelagola deserves a couple of hours to climb the two temple hills of Chandragiri and Vindhyagiri. The 57-feet tall monolithic statue of Lord Gomateshwara dwarfs everything around. Ideally, one should keep an entire day for the town as the walk up to the base of the mammoth statue can take a while to climb. The walk up on the rock-cut steps is exhausting and can be avoided by elderly people. (There are palanquins available for ₹200). Reach in time for the early morning prayers (8 a.m.) when devotees gather to chant together – a highly charged atmosphere envelopes the temple. Mahamastakabhisheka, a festival celebrated every 12 years, involves bathing the statue in consecrated water, milk, sugar cane juice and saffron paste. The next big day will be in 2018.

SECTION C
The Coastal Route (Mangaluru–Udipi–Jog Falls–Gokarna–Karwar)
ROAD CONDITION
The Mangaluru–Karwar Road that skirts the Arabian Sea is one of the key highways of Karnataka, also known as the Karavali region. Stretching from the southern edge of the state to the northernmost point along the coast, the road is scenic and dotted with a number of pit stops for the traveller. This is NH17, a single lane, which makes the traffic considerably slow. Expect to cover the 272-km stretch in not less than 7 hours. The condition of the road varies from season to season, the monsoons often posing a problem with large stretches of potholes and unpaved patches. While this along-the-coast highway is a treasure trove of scenic stops, the road condition makes it a task to manoeuvre.

EXPECTED SCENERY
One of the most stunning highways in the robust list of rich vistas in Karnataka, prepare to be mesmerized by the best of balmy coastal breeze as well as the million shades of green that lie on the other side of the road.

Flanked by these views, this road urges one to stop often for photo opportunities. A number of ancient temples also lie on this route, making it a busy stretch for devotees.

ESSENTIAL PIT STOPS

Udipi: This is one of the most significant stops on the Karavali region of Karnataka. Regarded as south India's holiest Vaishnavite centres with an enduring religious vibe, it is most famous for the Udipi festival when bulbous-domed chariots are hauled through the streets around the temple, which are dotted with *maths* (religious centres). Apart from the temples, the town is known for its dosas, St Mary's Island, beaches and a fabulous coin museum. The town requires more than just a day-long stop.

Mulki: Gaining ground on the travel sector, the village of Mulki is famous for India's first surfing set-up. This was established by Jack Hebner and Rick Perry, who surfed as kids and were among the pioneers of surfing in the East Coast of the USA. Tucked away in the inconspicuous coastal village, the surfing retreat, known as the Mantra Surf Club, is complemented by yoga, meditation, simple veg food and, of course, riding the waves.

Maravanthe & Other Beaches: Fishing villages and small towns along the coastal stretch of Mangaluru (earlier Mangalore) to Karwar are the unassuming delights of this route. Not shopworn with expected clichés, the offbeat tourist will love these. Many of the beaches are not developed for tourism and pleasantly retain the fishing culture. Three beaches worth your while are the Tannir Bavi Beach (8km from the city), Panambur (10km from Mangaluru) and Surathkal (14km). At any given time, there is no more than a handful of people here. Of these, Tannir Bavi has a huge parking area (₹20 for cars) and stone benches along the beach for you to sit and a few shops selling tea and snacks. Panambur, on the other hand, is slightly more action packed with plenty of snack shops, lifeguards, horse and camel rides and even some water-sports facilities during October–February. Surathkal is famous for its NITK lighthouse.

These beaches make for brilliant stops along the route but are unsafe for swimming.

Entry Fee: *Indians: ₹10, Children: ₹3, Foreigners: ₹25;* **Camera:** *₹20,* **Video:** *₹25;*
Timings: *4–5.30 p.m.*
The lighthouse is off limits during the monsoon months.

Experience Karnataka

Adrenalin rush: Water sports are popular among tourists visiting Karnataka

Closer to Udipi, Kaup (locally called Kapu) is tourist savvy with a few shops and the towering lighthouse as the key attraction. Mattu Beach (8.5km south of Udipi) is an elusive spot, not plagued by a surge of tourists. The access to this beach through a small bridge crossing the backwaters makes a scenic drive. Malpe (8km) is an energetic local tourist spot with a large parking, horse and camel rides, small food stalls and even water sports in non-monsoon months. Another attractive stop by the highway is Maravanthe Beach, which is especially scenic as the highway on this spot is flanked with the beach and the Souparnika River. Maravanthe is a great stop for a quick cup of tea and a view of waves lashing onto the shoreline. Baindur Beach is a dramatic rocky outcrop; you can follow the hillside along the beach and get a better viewing spot from the top.

Murudeshwar, a popular tourist beach, commands a vantage spot by the sea and is a stone's throw away from the famous Shiva temple of the same name. This is also the base point for a scuba-diving set-up that takes you to the Netrani Islands for a day-long, scuba-instructed trips.

SECTION D
Gorgeous Green (Bandipur–Kabini–Kodagu)
ROAD CONDITION

A number of roads radiate from Mysuru to the coveted travel destinations of Karnataka. The main exits include NH212 to south of Mysuru through Nanjanagudu to Bandipur and Masinagudi, towards the southwest to Kabini and the west to Kodagu via NH275. The single-laned roads are well maintained and a pleasure to drive on; the roads are dotted with small villages and forest patches in-between.

EXPECTED SCENERY

Bandipur, Kabini and Kodagu lie on the edge of the Western Ghats at the fringes of the Nilgiri Biosphere. This is one of the largest bio-diversity hotspots of southern India. Apart from the luscious green topography that you meet on the way, there are chances of running into wildlife. Nilgais and elephants are common sightings on these roads.

> **ALERT:** The road to Bandipur is closed at night, between 6 p.m. and 6 a.m., so avoid taking an overnight drive. Animal crossings are common in the region.

ESSENTIAL PIT STOPS

Bylakuppe: This Tibetan settlement lies just on the western edge of Mysuru district, bordering Kodagu – a must-vist for the Namdroling Monastery. Established by Lugsum Samdupling in 1961 and further complemented by Dickyi Larsoe in 1969, the Tibetan settlement at Bylakuppe seems incongruous to Kodagu's cultural identity but ushers in the diversity for Karnataka.

SECTION E
Coffee & Treks (Hassan–Chikmagalur)
ROAD CONDITION

Hassan is the veritable base for the Hoysala cluster of temples around Belur and Halebeedu. This is also the town, which is a nodal junction on way to Chikmagalur. The four-lane highway from Bengaluru to Hassan shrinks to a single road via Belur to Chikmagalur, but the stretch is impeccable. Smooth, clear roads allow the driver to complete the distance in a short span. It is the road from Belur to Chikmagalur that is riddled with a few irregular and pot-holed patches but nothing of great concern. The 60-km stretch from Hassan to Chikmagalur is best done via the Belur Road and SH57.

EXPECTED SCENERY

The road from Hassan to Chikmagalur is characteristic of the Karnataka countryside with green fields and small hamlets dotting the topography. Miles of swaying fields as far as your eyes can see flank the smooth road.

ESSENTIAL PIT STOPS

Gorur Dam: Located 9km outside Hassan, the Gorur Dam is built on the Hemavathi River. The gates of the dam are opened after the monsoons, which is an ideal time to visit the spot. A thundering wall of water gushes out of the gate, forming a misty white halo along the ledge of the dam. After a

Experience Karnataka

Gorur Dam, across Hemavathy River, is a popular tourist destination

long walk to the dam area from the gate, one can go pretty close to see the water. The dam is opened from 10 a.m.–5 p.m. on all days.

SECTION F
Sylvan Track (Shimoga–Hubli/Dharwad–Dandeli)
ROAD CONDITION
The Shimoga–Hubli/Dharwad–Dandeli stretch, of about 400km that runs parallel to the coast of Karnataka, brings in an alternate cultural aspect of the state. The route is mapped along NH4 for most part of the sector, with good roads with a few ghat sections that add to the drive.

EXPECTED SCENERY
Except for the ghat sections near Ranebenur off Davangere, a large part of the route lies along the plains of Karnataka. Expect sprawling fields on either side of the road, and small hamlets dotting the road.

> **TOP TIP:** Hubli, Davangere and Dharwad are busy junctions, being major towns, so avoiding the main town to catch the bypass is always recommended.

SECTION G
History Unravelled (Badami–Pattadakal–Aihole–Hampi)
ROAD CONDITION
Keeping Hampi as the base, you can also cover the central cultural circuit of

Pattadakal, Badami and Aihole. The route is chalked along NH13, making it a smooth ride. The roads with the triangle of Pattadakal, Badami and Aihole, leave some room for improvement.

EXPECTED SCENERY

The stark weather-beaten topography offers a palate of browns for the eyes. Still, the rockscape is mesmerizing, especially with a few patches of fresh green just after the monsoon.

Durga Temple in Aihole was built by the Chalukyas between 7-8th centuries

SECTION H
Stories in Stones (Vijayapura–Bidar)
ROAD CONDITION

A feast for the eyes because of its architectural splendour, Vijayapura (earlier Bijapur) is more than 500km from Bengaluru. Although best reached by train, you can drive to Vijayapura from Bengaluru via NH4 and NH13 that cuts across the state. In-between Vijayapura and Bidar lies Basavakalyan, from where you can plan your trips to each city to soak in the majestic monuments, and pick up a few *bidri* handicrafts from Bidar.

EXPECTED SCENERY

The road from Vijayapura to Bidar is pretty stark. The basalt rock topography offers shades of brown all around, which, in spite of being bare, has an appeal of its own.

ESSENTIALS FOR YOUR TRIP

Amongst other cities in Karnataka, Bengaluru boasts close proximity to a wide range of destinations, making 'weekend travel' extremely popular in the state. It is equipped with reasonably good infrastructure on the highways for those keen on road travel and self driving. However, some essentials are imperative to tick in your checklist before getting started.

Planning

Amongst the steps to plan your travel, chalking out a viable route, pit stops and total time spent on the road are bare essentials. Knowing your choices for roads is the first thing that you must do. Season plays an integral part of the planning procedure. This could include the affability towards rains, travelling in summers or winters, timings of resorts which might create difficulties for a particular season, or festivals. For example, the Neelakurinji flowers that bloom every 12 years are found in the Shola forests of the Western Ghats. One is likely to see them in places like Munnar, Kodagu and Chikmagalur. Plan ahead – the next time the flower will blossom will be in 2018.

Know your Roads

Driving for long hours can be taxing and it is important to know the environment you will be encountering, especially the Ghats (mountain) and wildlife sections, where roads can be blocked for long hours during the nights.

Driving in Karnataka means that one would hit some amount of mountainous regions, especially towards the Nilgiris. Use lower gears to manoeuvre the winding roads and always look out for any burning smell – it could be the brake or the clutch. Stay on your side. Sleep well the night before; try and head out early in the morning for better visibility.

With national parks and tiger reserves like Bandipur, Mudumalai and Wayanad of the Nilgiri Biosphere, there is bound to be some spillover of wildlife onto the highways when the animals are crossing roads. Though many of these highways are closed at nights, evenings are a sensitive time for visibility. Be very alert and keep eyes wide open for deer, wild boar, sambhars and snakes on the roads.

KEY HIGHWAY EXITS FROM BENGALURU

Bengaluru has five major exits on National and State Highways:
NH4: Pune–Bengaluru (Tumkur Road)
NH7: Hyderabad–Bengaluru (Hosur Road)
NH48: Hassan–Bengaluru
NH209: Kanakapura–Bengaluru
SH17: Mysuru–Bengaluru (Mysore Road)

NICE Road

The Nandi Infrastructure Corridor Enterprises Limited (NICE) is a 4–6 lane expressway – tolled-fenced road – that was developed to connect Bengaluru to Mysuru to alleviate the traffic congestion in south Bengaluru. The road also exits on NH7 (Hosur Road) at Electronic City, NH4 (Tumkur Road) near Nelamangala, Banerghatta Road within Bengaluru, NH209 (Kanakapura Road) and SH17 (Mysore Road).

Getting your Car or Bike Ready

Ensure that your tool kit, documents, hazard indicator, spare tyre, coolant and oils are in place before you head out on a long drive. Most cars and bikes supply a suggested tyre pressure limit for highways, which is different from daily use – get this checked just a day before you leave. Tyres checked for air is imperative – and so is an emergency contact list for mechanics. Invest in a ready-to-use puncture liquid for emergencies, which will see you through till you find a mechanic on the road.

What to Pack

While there can never be a comprehensive packing list, listing down some requisites will come in handy.

- A light all-weather jacket as places in Karnataka tend to get windy or cold even with a light shower.
- Crocs or similar open shoes that can resist water – hopping over streams and long walks will be easier. Pack closed trekking shoes or sneakers for something more intensive.
- Sunscreen for the tropical weather, especially for the summer months of March and April.
- Packets of dry foods like biscuits and water for long stretches on the road.
- Though chemists are not difficult to find in Karnataka's towns, handy and specific medicines for illnesses is recommended.
- Soft, cotton tees and full-length pants are recommended for temple pit stops.
- A scarf that works as a head/nose cover to protect from sun and dust.
- Sunglasses to protect the eyes.

Getting Acquainted with Karnataka

Karnataka marks the transition area between central India and the Dravidian South, giving it a unique vantage position of 'best of both worlds'. An inexhaustible goldmine of nature, culture and art, the state is sure to leave you enthralled. You will find stark differences in the northern and southern belts, making it an interesting state for varied travel experiences. Apart from regional diversity, Karnataka boasts diverse topography, historical relics and modern entertainment, asserting itself as one of the most exquisite destinations in south India.

Partially along the northern and more on the eastern edge of the state, one can find traces of an erstwhile Mughal stronghold, now depicted in domed mausoleums and minarets of Vijayapura (earlier Bijapur) and Bidar. Along the western edge of the state lie the Western Ghats range of mountains and untreaded coastal delights that offer contrasting topography to the rest of the state. While hues of green and an abundance of tropical forests, avian and wildlife make this a paradise, the hidden sandy stretches along the coast of Karnataka offer unparalleled experiences of water-based adventure and a soothing, pleasing view. The simple life of fishermen is what draws many to the western edge of Karnataka. The Western Ghats of India is one of the wettest regions and a UNESCO World Heritage Site. Considered one of the eight hotspots of biological diversity in the world, these stretch down to Kerala in the south.

The central part of the state is dotted with ruins of the Vijayanagar kingdom in Hampi, a period remembered by its near-ruined temples and derelict palaces that rise from the arid, rocky landscape in surreal beauty. The rest of the central region too is baked dry, given that it forms a part of the Mysore Plateau. The only relief that the region sees is by way of the two

◀ The Sringa, a musical instrument, is a type of horn played during rituals

capillaries on the map: the Tungabhadra and Krishna rivers that flow across this terrain, finally draining east to the Bay of Bengal. Talking of rivers, the Cauvery and Kali are also major water lifelines of the state.

On the south lies the bastion of development, Bengaluru. The capital city, formerly known as Bangalore, epitomizes the aspirations and growth that has swept the city since the IT boom. The state's second-most important city, Mysuru, is known for its Raj-esque era, nineteenth-century palaces and silk and incense markets.

A cluster of un-missable sights present themselves all over the state. Kodagu, Shravanabelagola, Pattadakal, Badami, Aihole, Sakleshpur, Gokarna, Jog Falls and Udipi are names that feature high on a tourist's list.

A BRIEF HISTORY OF KARNATAKA

The history of Karnataka, like much of south India, can be traced back to influences and rule by Buddhist, Hindu and Muslim dynasties. Jainism also had a deep impact on the state. Chandragupta Maurya (340–298 BC) is believed to have converted to Jainism in the fourth century BC. He then renounced his throne and fasted to death at Shravanabelagola, now one of the most-visited Jain pilgrimage centres in the country. Chalukyas, Cholas, Gangas, Hoysalas and the Vijayanagar kingdom dominated the power struggles of the Deccan over the centuries, fractured by Muslim invasions from time to time. The most significant capital, Vijayanagar, stretched from the Bay of Bengal to the Arabian Sea and south to Cape Comorin but lost to the superior military strength of the Bahamani dynasty in 1565 at the Battle of Talikota. The region never did recover from the plundering. While the Muslims held away in the north, the Wodeyar rajas of Mysore kept their territory intact in the south. It was in 1761 that the Muslim leader Hyder Ali, with French support, seized the throne. Thus began a period of great upliftment in Karnataka as his son, Tipu Sultan, turned Mysore into a major force in the south before the British killed him in the Battle of Srirangapatnam, in 1799. Colonial rule followed for the next half century, until the merging of the states of Mysore and the Madras Presidencies in 1956 created Karnataka.

GETTING THERE

The two international airports, Kempegowda in Bengaluru (www.bengaluruairport.com) and Mangalore International Airport (formerly Bajpe Airport), are the two leading nodal junctions to reach the state by air. The two cities are well connected by domestic and international flights. In fact, Kempegowda International Airport, Bengaluru, clocked 15 million passengers in 2014-15. It is now south India's busiest airport and India's third-largest base. Bengaluru is often seen as the gateway to south India, given its proximity and access to many significant cities. Other notable airports lie in Belgaum, Hubli and Mysuru, connecting the smaller sightseeing circuits to the rest of the country. Limited air carriers operate at these junctions.

Karnataka's rail network overlaps the western and southern sectors, connecting major and small cities of India to its many junctions. Coastal Karnataka is covered under the Konkan railway network, given the feasibility of direction and area assigned. The main station of the capital city is Bengaluru City Railway Station (SBC; its name was officially changed to Krantivira Sangolli Rayanna in 2015), which is complemented by Yesvantpur (YPR) and Bengaluru Cantt (BNC) stations to ply hundreds of trains from and through the city. While the rest of the state is well connected, the hill regions of Chikmagalur and Kodagu are not yet connected by train.

THE GOLDEN CHARIOT

The Golden Chariot, a luxury train operated by the Tourism Department of Karnataka, rolls on to the places of interest in Karnataka and Goa under the tour name 'Pride of the South'. It covers Bengaluru–Kabini/ Bandipur–Mysuru–Hassan–Hampi– Gadag–Goa–Bengaluru. The same train covers places of interest in Karnataka, Tamil Nadu, Kerala with a different tour name: 'Southern Splendour'. In this, the places covered are Bengaluru–Chennai– Mamallapuram–Pondicherry– Tiruchirapalli & Thanjavur–Madurai– Kanyakumari–Thiruvananthapuram –Backwaters & Kochi/Allepey– Bengaluru.

The train offers 18 coaches with fully equipped rooms, traditional decor, delicious food and exemplary service.

Over 27 national highways and more state highways criss-cross in Karnataka, making it one of the most conducive destinations for road travel. This also means that the highways are well equipped with pit stops along the way to rest and eat. The Karnataka State Road Transport Corporation (KSRTC), an efficient service that has been operational for more than fifty years, manages the public bus transport in Karnataka. Fleets of private, high-end AC buses with push-back seats operate within and across borders to Kerala, Andhra Pradesh, Telangana and Tamil Nadu. Overnight travel optimizes time and is a convenient option for road travellers. Self-driving is a popular choice given the good roads and dynamic scenery across the state.

BEST SEASON

There is hardly any period that is not appropriate for travelling to Karnataka.

October–March

This is the best season to spot tigers, leopards and elephants in Karnataka's pristine national parks or opt for the temple trails. This is also the time for the annual Hampi festival. October marks the Dusshera celebrations in Mysuru with night-long festivities and the majestic jumbo parades. December is the best period to get respite from the heat, making it easier to explore the region's fabulous forts, palaces, caves and temples.

March-April

These are the hottest months in Karnataka, with temperatures soaring higher every year. The monsoons are not everyone's favourite, but the rains do add a cathartic touch to the Western Ghats, draping it in a million shades of green – for some this is hardly a deterrent.

FAIRS AND FESTIVALS

Being the multi-cultural state that it is, there are a number of fairs and festivals that are celebrated through the year in Karnataka. The top five festivals of the state have been given below.

Mysore Dusshera

With a history of more than 400 years, the Mysore Dusshera is the most significant festival of the state. It is also known as the 'Nadahabba' or the State Festival. This is a ten-day celebration headed by the royal family of Mysuru, and refers to the ten-day festival with the last day being Vijayadashami. This is the most auspicious day of Dusshera and denotes the victory of truth over evil – it was the day when Goddess Chamundeshwari killed the demon Mahishasura. (Incidentally, the name of Mysuru has been derived from the name 'Mahishasura'.) The main attraction of the festival lies in the lighting up of the Mysore Palace and the cultural parades that are held during the day.

Ugaadi

An important festival in Karnataka, Ugaadi is the New Year's Day for the people of the region. It is also celebrated with intense fervour in Andhra Pradesh, Telangana, Goa and Maharashtra. Bevu-Bella, the act of eating six different types of dishes, symbolizes the fact that life is a mixture of different experiences, namely sadness, happiness, anger, fear, disgust and surprise. Eating a specific mixture of six tastes, called Ugaadi Pachhadi, symbolizes this thought. It consists of neem (bitterness and sadness), jaggery (happiness), green chilli/pepper (anger), salt (fear), tamarind (disgust) and unripened mango (surprise). Another special dish called Holige (roti and jaggery) is prepared on this day. The festival is not only a celebration of New Year's Day but a day to pray for blessings and general well-being.

Nrityotsava

The ancient Chalukyan capital and World Heritage Centre, Pattadakal, comes alive in January each year with the annual dance festival, Nrityotsava. It draws famous dancers from all over the world. Pattadakal is known for its intricately carved temples that represent the north and south Indian architectural traditions. This dance festival is organized by the Karnataka government against the backdrop of these festivals to celebrate the heritage of the state.

Ganesh Habba

Ganesha Chaturthi is celebrated as the day on which Ganesha, the Elephant God, son of Shiva and Parvathi, resurrected to life on earth. The birthday of Lord Ganesha throws Karnataka into frenzy, when people pray to colourfully painted clay idols of Ganesha for a period of ten days. The installation of the idol in homes and residential complexes overrides everything else during the Chaturthi days. Temporary *mantapas* (pandals) are erected in every locality. Decorations include flowers, small banana saplings, lights, etc., or now theme-based decorations, which depict religious themes or current events. The celebrations go on for ten days, from Bhadrapad Shudh Chaturthi to the Ananta Chaturdashi. On the eleventh day, the statue is taken in a procession accompanied with dancing and singing to be immersed in a water body.

Hampi Utsav

Hampi's annual festival takes place in the month of December or January to commemorate the heritage, lineage and cultural ambience of the destination. Various artistes of national and international repute participate in the festival, where dance and music are the highlights. Fireworks, folk dances, drama, puppet shows and even mud wrestling have been incorporated over the years.

Dosas by the dozen, being cooked at a roadside restaurant

CUISINE

The distinct regional culinary traditions of Karnataka are as varied as the scape of the state. Kannada fare is considered one of the oldest surviving cuisines and traces its origin to the Iron Age. Bisi Bele Bhath, Jolada Rotti, Chapati, Ragi Rotti, Akki Rotti, Saaru, Idli-Vada-Sambar combination, Vangi Bhath, Khara Bhath, Kesari Bhath, Davangere Benne Dosa, Ragi Mudde, Paddu/Gundponglu, Koli Saaru (chicken curry), Maamsa Saaru (mutton curry), and Uppittu are names that one gets to hear regularly in the kitchens of the state. The ubiquitous Masala Dosa traces its roots to Udipi. Kodagu has been responsible for tickling the taste buds for non-vegetarians with excellent Pandi Curry (pork). Each region offers a distinct style and platter of cuisines. Malenad, Mangalorean and Navayath regions bring definitive flavours and styles of cooking to the table, other than the generic Kannada dishes. A collection of varied flavours and ingredients from the coastal border to the inlands, and the hilly plantations, Karnataka offers ample choices for the foodie and a fresh sample for your senses to relish.

MUSIC

Karnataka has adopted both the Hindustani and Carnatic styles of music, though traditionally Carnatic music has left a firmer footprint in the cultural scape of the state. When Vaishnavism and the Haridasa movement started influencing the state, the musical environment offered a haven for artistes like Purandaradasa, whose use of the local Kannada language appealed to the masses. A wandering bard, it is said that he has composed 75,000–4,75,000 songs in Sanskrit and Kannada. It was clear, devotionally inclined and had a touch of philosophy. Other names that remain deeply entrenched in memory are Kanakadasa, Vyasatirtha, Jayatirtha, Sripadaraya and Vadirajatirtha, amongst others. The era between the fifteenth and sixteenth centuries influenced and inspired names like Tyagaraja to take on the baton. Once the musical environment pulsated in the state, future centuries only nourished the Carnatic music scene for other artistes.

Some of the most impactful names of Hindustani music also came from Karnataka. Gangubai Hangal, Puttaraj Gawai, Pt Bhimsen Joshi, Pt Mallikarjun Mansur, Basavaraj Rajguru, Sawai Gandharva and Kumar Gandharva have left an indelible mark in this sphere.

Gangubai Hangal was a renowned Hindustani classical vocalist

TRADITIONAL DANCE FORMS

Karnataka's dance forms have always appealed to the tourist. Each region has a definitive segmentation by the dresses and types of dance. Some of the major dance forms of the state are given below.

Aati Kalanja

This is a ritualistic folk dance performed by the Nalke community of coastal Karnataka. Kalanja is the name of a protector spirit of the village folk during the month of July-August. The dancers wear a costume made of tender coconut leaves, anklets, colourful cloth, a long cap and paint their faces with bright colours. An umbrella made of leaves and decorated with

Experience Karnataka

leaves and flowers are the main props of the dance. Going from house to house, the artiste dances and blesses the family members for which he is given paddy, rice, coconut, turmeric and charcoal. The other members of the group sing the story of the spirit in the background to the beat of a small drum known as *tembere*.

Bhutha Kola

This is one of the most well-known dances of the coastal Tulunadu region (southern Karnataka, bordering Kerala), where a divine spirit is said to enter the body of the dancer, and ushers him into a hypnotic performance. There are about 350 *bhuthas* (spirits) in the Canara region. The ritualistic dance is performed during the end of the year to the tune of epics and folk songs sung in the paddy plantation field by the women folk. The *maadira* dance is related to the Bhutha Kola. When the women folk of the community of Bhutha dancers are free in the rainy season, they go out in pairs, dancing to the beat of a small drum, often singing about love and marriage.

Yakshagana performance, depicts stories from epic poems and the Puranas

Yakshagana

A folk composition that synthesizes dance, music, dialogue, costume, make-up, and stage techniques, the origins of this dance form lies somewhere between the sixteenth and the eighteenth centuries. It was strongly influenced by the Bhakti movement. It is now performed in the coastal regions of Karnataka in the latter part of the year, from dusk to dawn. Male actors play the roles of women as well, while a group of musicians play the background score. The music is based on ragas, which are characterized by rhythmic beats. The themes of this dance-drama are derived from epics and ancient Hindu texts. Similar to Yakshagana, Doddata is the name given to a similar folk performance in the northern part of the state.

Kamsale

Popular in southern parts of the state, like Mysuru, Nanjangudu, Kollegal and Bengaluru, Kamsale is named after the instrument that is played during the performance. Slightly acrobatic in nature, men dance to the rhythmic clang of a *kamsale*, a cymbal-metal disc combination. The dance is performed by the Haalu Kuruba community, who have vowed to live a life of devotion to Lord Mahadeeshvara, a form of Lord Shiva.

Bolak Aat

Endemic to the Kodagu region, the history of this dance can be traced to a legend in which Lord Vishnu took various avatars for the destruction of the demon Bhasmasura. He performed thirty varieties of dance, of which one is the Bolak. This dance is performed in front of an oil lamp in an open field, exclusively by men in the traditional *kodava* dress. A *chavari* (yak-fur) and a *kodava katti* (sickle) are the main props used in this dance form.

Gorava Nrithya

A dance performed by the devotees of Shiva, this is popular in Mysuru and north Karnataka regions. The *goravas* (dancers) wear colourful costumes and hold a *damaru* (percussion instrument) and *pillangoovi* (flute). The devotees dance in a trance, sometimes even barking like dogs. It is believed that the emblem of the Mylaralinga, a form of Shiva, is a dog. There is no fixed choreography to this dance.

Jaggahalige Kunitha

The *jaggahalige* is a percussion instrument made of a bullock cartwheel, wrapped in buffalo hide. On Holi (March) and Ugaadi (regional New Year), villages in the Dharwad region roll a dozen giant instruments and conduct a procession. Beats of the instrument waft through the villages as the procession makes way. Joodu Haligi is a variation of this with only two percussionists on the job.

Dollu Kunitha

One of the most popular folk dances of the state, one gets to see many variations of the Dollu Kunitha. Dollu is a percussion instrument used in the group dance of the Kuruba community of north Karnataka. A group of 16

Experience Karnataka

Artistes performing Dollu Kunitha, for the presiding deity of Beereshwara or Beeralingeswara

dancers beat the drum and dance to its rhythms – they are directed by a leader with cymbals, who moves only in the centre. Slow and fast rhythms alternate as the dance troupe weaves different formations.

Karangolu
A harvest dance that can be seen in the months of January and February, Karangolu offers a celebratory tinge to the lives of the Harijan community. Dressed up as an old man or a woman, the artiste holds a stick and beats a drum, while dancing from house to house to receive alms.

Kombat
Popular in the Kodagu region, this temple dance has found its way out of the premises and into the community. Men dancing, holding deer horns, is the main attraction of this dance.

Suggi Kunitha
The festival dance of Haalakki Vakkaliga performed by men during the harvest season is known as Suggi Kunitha. Popular in north coastal Karnataka, the festival begins in March and the dance starts on a full moon

day. Characters dress up as clowns or minor comics to complement the main dancers who wear an elaborate headgear.

Ummattat

Exclusively performed by Coorgi women, this dance entails rhythmic steps by ladies as one of them stands with a pot full of water, representing the deity Kaveri. The legend of this dance is connected to the story of Vishnu in the guise of Mohini.

Veeragase

This ritualistic dance is connected to Shiva, where groups of two, four or six pierce long and short needles across their mouths and dance to the tempo of percussions and cymbals.

Kudubi Holi (Tribal Dance)

The tribal community of Kudubi is settled near the northern coastal Karnataka belt. On the day of Holi, men dance in a semicircle to the beat of a *gummate* (percussion instrument). This traditional dance marks the blend of Marathi culture in this region.

Colourfully dressed, each dancer of Kudubi Holi holds a *gummate*, a percussion instrument

Bheemeshwari, a scenic spot on the river Cauvery, is a perfect getaway

NATURE AND OUTDOORS

Karnataka's stupendous natural wealth is the largest draw for many travellers. From the gushing rivers that offer a chance to raft down their frothy curves to the dizzying mountain-tops that one can climb, the state is a treasure trove for outdoor enthusiasts. The lush band of palm trees along the coast stands in deep contrast to the stark colours of Hampi and around, and yet the two harmonize to make the state one of the richest in scapes. The Western Ghats with its Nilgiri Biosphere is one of the richest in flora and fauna, giving the nature lover the opportunity to explore the region with alacrity. Scenic vistas apart, the coffee plantations of Kodagu, Chikmagalur and Sakleshpur leave an indelible mark in the minds of travellers with vast scope of learning about the natural heritage of the regions.

ART AND CULTURE

Karnataka's enduring cultural appeal lies in its deep roots of folk history and a strong connect with traditions. Leather puppets, giant dolls called *gaarudi gombe* and other folk performances like public narratives set in the villages are still prevalent in the state. Other interesting aspects like the act of miming by *hagalu veshagaararu* (day actors) is something only seen in parts of Karnataka and Andhra Pradesh. Folk orchestras form another dimension to the art and culture of the state. These are known as 'Karadimajal'. The tradition of ballads called *laavani*, can still be seen in Karnataka.

SPECIAL FOCUS

Two of the state's largest contributors to traveller needs are the Karnataka State Road Transportation Corporation (KSRTC) and the Jungle Lodges & Resort (JLR). These two establishments have consistently improved access to different travel destinations of the state, with safe and affordable services in the field of transportation and accommodation. KSRTC has facilitated road travel by offering a robust and affordable time-table of buses across Karnataka and adjoining states. The high-end buses are very comfortable and have a wide range in terms of prices. There are some that give blankets, snacks, water bottles, etc., as well. There are cheaper ones too, which don't have the frills but are safe and popular. The best place to book is at www.ksrtc.in

Karnataka State Road Transportation Corporation

It was the year 1948, when 120 buses formed the first fleet of buses that would ply in the state boundary to transfer public. Established by the then state of Mysore as the Mysore Government Road Transport Department

The majestic bus terminus of the KSRTC

(MGRTD), the company has grown in leaps and bounds, and now stands as the skeleton of road transportation in the state. Over the years, the outfit has graduated to offer air-conditioned Volvo buses that ply from a number of major and smaller towns within and to the adjoining states of Karnataka. Reasonably priced, the vast choice of fares and routes gives a traveller the access to several destinations. Operating in seven districts, KSRTC has a fleet of more than 8,000 buses and caters to a whopping 29-lakh-plus passengers on a daily basis.

Jungle Lodges & Resorts

Holding the baton for being one of the best eco-tourism establishments in the state, Jungle Lodges & Resorts (JLR) properties are ones that regulars will swear by. It was the Kabini Lodge in 1980 that paved the way for 15 others over the years with its impeccable hospitality and grand location. Being a part-government entity, vantage locations and access to natural water bodies and forests are the highlights of the JLR properties. Add to that the amenities, facilities and insightful local knowledge and even the best properties cannot rule the hospitality scape. From well-appointed rooms in different categories to the simple food and activities, JLR has broken the mould where affordable state-run properties are concerned. JLR offers admirable experiences in Kabini, BR Hills, Bheemeshwari, Galibore, Dandeli, Karwar, Banerghatta, Bandipur, Lakavalli, Ganesh Gudi, Pilikula Nisargadhama, Hampi and Bidar.

Jungle Lodges & Resorts offer interesting staying options throughout Karnataka

Popular choice: JLR cottages in sylvan setting

Small Companies, Big Dreams

Tailor-made trips, niche experiences and exceptional local insights have been the mantra for the last decade in travel. Karnataka's composition of travellers have received this well and continue to do so as boutique holidaymakers embellish their plans with off-beat, relatively untreaded and experiential additions. Some of the names that have cropped up in the last few years and before are Nirvana Nomads, Motorcycle Travellers Meet, Toehold, Thrillophilia, Exotic Expeditions, Darter Photography, and Bangalore Walks along with more. The start-up culture of the capital city has rubbed off on travel as well, offering tourists a number of options to fill their weekends.

Bengaluru

Folk artistes at the Bangalore Palace

A Deccan destination that is hard to ignore, Bengaluru is bound to rank high with a discerning traveller who will appreciate its heady cosmopolitan identity and still be able to step back in time to explore its Hindu, Mughal and colonial ties. Bengaluru's reputation of a city with a vibrant pub culture and ever-pleasant weather precedes itself and are the winning highlights of the city that makes it an ideal base to discover parts of Kerala, Tamil Nadu, Goa, Telangana and Andhra Pradesh – all falling only a couple of hours drive away from the city. Bengaluru has held the baton for being the perfect centre point for weekend getaways in the entire country. The accessibility and infrastructure put it in good stead with those who are keen on discovering Bengaluru by driving in and around the city. You will find most people referring to it by its former name, Bangalore, even though in November 2014, its name was officially changed to Bengaluru to fade its colonial tinge and return to more ethnic lineage.

Founded by Kempe Gowda, the city was enclosed within four cardinal towers in 1537. One of the towers lies atop a hillock in Lal Bagh, the second

Experience Karnataka

at the edge of Ulsoor Lake, one hidden near Kempambudhi Lake (close to the Bandi Mahakali Temple at Hanumanthanagar) and the last one stands near the Mekhri Circle underpass in a well-maintained park. But the history of Bengaluru was shaped by a series of events post-Kempe Gowda rule. The current cultural and social tapestry of the city is coloured by its Hindu, Mughals and British lineage. It started when Kempe Gowda's waning hold on the city since 1537 made him transfer hands to the father–son duo Hyder Ali–Tipu Sultan, and eventually to the Britishers in the late eighteenth century. The mixed history gives the city its cosmopolitan vibe till date. You will find that modern Bengaluru is a mosaic of a pulsating culture of pubs, love for music, food, art, culture and tradition. Though it has an energetic ambience, the city draws you with ease into its easy paced life; the cool pleasant weather doing its bit, too. What is most striking here is the strong sense of collective conscience of the community. Groups like the Ugly Indian organizing spot cleaning on the streets or a recycling–reuse drive through households and many such socially relevant projects are abundant in the city. The IT connect of 'India's Silicon Valley' stature cannot be missed, neither can its status as the best city for start-ups. In fact, one particular road has also been christened 'Start Up Gali'.

Bengaluru's urban charm is a function of its endless commotion with ever-increasing traffic, entrepreneurial hue and deep-rooted history. It is a city that is hard to ignore and easy to fall in love with.

EXPLORING THE CITY
Acclimatization with Walks and Day Trips

A vast history, cultural influences and the contemporary status of a city are hard to absorb unless you get a quick insider's view. Bangalore Walks makes this simple by offering well-constructed, 'easy on the legs' walking tours of the city. The Victorian Bangalore Walk is particularly popular, and takes you down the small stretch of barely 2km from Trinity Church, covering East Parade Church, landmark buildings and monuments like Mayo Hall, Utility Building and Kittel's Statue on MG Road, ending in breakfast at the Barton Centre on the arterial Mahatma Gandhi Road. Sprinkled with numerous anecdotes, the walk is one of the best experiences of the city. This is also a good way to see Lal Bagh, Basavanagudi and the old city areas.

Ph: 09845523660;
www.bangalorewalks.com;
Cost: *Approx. ₹500 per head.*

Trouping along the streets of Bengaluru is made much more fun

Art of Bicycle Trips trundles up to Nandi Hills, a popular day tour among tourists

by folks on spokes, called Art of Bicycle Trips, or AoBT. What started as a few day trips by AoBT, is now zooming in many parts of the world, but their heart still lies in Bengaluru, where it all started. Sign up for day-long trips or a few hours, depending on time and inclination to pedal away.

Ph: 07899437583;
www.artofbicycletrips.com;
Cost: *Half-day tour is ₹3,000 per head, for a group of 4 or more/full-day tour, ₹4,800 per head for a group of 4 or more.*

Unhurried epitomizes the need to see a city at your own pace, slowly soaking in the wonders. Join the walking tours for a peek into the heritage and cultural nuances of the city. The signature walks around the Malleshwaram, Russel Market, Fraser Town and Johnson Market areas is what put Unhurried on the map. Once you've had a taste of one sojourn, you will definitely come back for more.

Ph: 9880565446; www.unhurried.in;
Cost: *Approx. ₹1,299 per head.*

Indian National Trust for Art and Cultural Heritage (INTACH) also actively organizes trawls around the city. The Devanhalli, Sultanpet and Nandi walks out of an array of others are highly recommended to immerse yourself in the history of Bengaluru.

166, Kathriguppe Water Tank Road, 4th Cross, Banashankari 3rd Stage, Bengaluru; Ph: 080-26794220; www.intachblr.org;
Cost: *₹100 or ₹120 per head (depending on the walk and place); look out for free walks sometimes.*

Experience Karnataka

SIGHTSEEING HIGHLIGHTS
National Gallery of Modern Art

The National Gallery of Modern Art (NGMA) in Bengaluru has found home in a 100-year-old restored heritage building, surrounded by gigantic shady trees, fountains and gardens. The gallery hosts the work of eminent artists, workshops, film screenings, talks and events around music, theatre and dance. Free instructed walks, 'Introduction to the language of visual art' (**Timings**: Wednesdays, 3 p.m.) and 'Introduction to Modern Indian Art' (**Timings**: Saturdays, 10.30 a.m.) and regular shows are on the cards.

49, Palace Road, Vasanthanagar, Bengaluru; Ph: 080-22342338; www.ngmaindia.gov.in; **Entry Fee**: *Indians:₹10, Children:₹1, Foreigners:₹150;* **Timings**: *10 a.m.–5 p.m.; Closed on Mondays and National Holidays.*

Bangalore Boulevard

The much-needed arrival of the Bangalore Metro service also brought with it the heartache of a changing topography. The iconic MG Road, in particular, went through a massive change: 6 May 2013 saw the arrival of the restored MG Road after the green boulevard on the opposite side of shops was disfigured by metro construction. Now a two-tiered pathway with a gallery, shops, childrens' play area, artisans' hub and even a friendship-band tying corner stretches along for 500 metres below the metro and is christened the Rangoli Metro Art Centre.

Boulevard, MG Road, Bengaluru; **Timings**: *10 a.m.–7 p.m.*

A puppet show at NGMA during the Dhaatu International Puppet Festival

The majestic Bangalore Palace is a must-see in the tourists' itinerary

Bangalore Palace

Rising from a dusty brown expanse of land, the ivy-clad Bangalore Palace is one of the most iconic structures of the city. It was constructed by Rev. Garett and is now owned by the Mysore royal family. Supposedly designed after the Windsor Castle in London, it requires a few hours of your time. Take the audio tour of the ballroom on the ground floor and the elaborate Durbar Hall on the first, packed with paintings, artefacts, mounted animal heads and more for an immersive experience. A horse carriage ride around the palace grounds in an old buggy is also available.

1, Palace Road, Vasanthanagar, Bengaluru; Ph: 080-23360818; **Entry Fee**: Indians: ₹225, Foreigners: ₹450; **Camera**: ₹675, **Cell phone photography**: ₹280; **Timings**: 10 a.m.–5.30 p.m.

ISKCON Temple

The International Society for Krishna Consciousness (ISKCON) Temple is a milky white sprawling complex, which engulfs hundreds in its spiritual vibe each day. Founded by AC Bhaktivedanta Swami Prabhupada, to promote Vedic culture and spiritual learning, the society is spread all over the world. In Bengaluru too, it is run with meticulous precision, despite the hoards of devotees that come to visit its ten temples and an eatery (**Timings**: 7.30 a.m.–2 p.m., 4.30–9 p.m.). Strains of *Hare Rama, Hare Krishna* make a constant backdrop to your visit.

West Chord Road, Hare Krishna Hall, 1st Block, Rajaji Nagar, Bengaluru;
Ph: 080-23471956;
www.iskonbangalore.org; **Timings**: *4.15–5 a.m., 7.15 a.m.–12.50 p.m., 4–8.20 p.m.*

Banerghatta National Park

Banerghatta National Park lies 22km off Bengaluru, and is the closest place for that dose of the wild. You cannot ignore the slightly packaged-tour feel to the trip. Avoid weekends if you can – the place is jostling with visitors. The canter safari takes you through a small section of the 104-sqkm park and, if you are lucky, you can spot bison, bears and deer; tigers are usually caged. You are more likely to satisfy yourself with the inhabitants of the zoo and a butterfly park – the first ever in India. Those travelling with children may enjoy this more.

Ph: 080-22352828;
Entry Fee: *₹50,* **Safari + Zoo**: *₹210,*
Butterfly Park: *₹20;* **Camera**: *₹25,*
Video: *₹110;*
Timings: *9 a.m.–5 p.m., Grand Safari: 11 a.m.–4 p.m.; Tuesdays closed.*

Parks of Bengaluru

The dwindling greenscape of the city is redeemed by the two major parks of the city: Lal Bagh Botanical Gardens and Cubbon Park off MG Road. Spread over 240 acres, Lal Bagh was commissioned by Hyder Ali (later completed under Tipu Sultan's rule) in 1760. With one of the largest collections of rare botanical gems, the highlights of the park include a glasshouse, one of the four towers placed by Kempe Gowda – the founder of the city – and a hillock made up of a 3,000 million-year-old peninsular gneissic rock. Apart from regular fitness enthusiasts in the mornings and tourists, an annual flower show in January draws thousands to Lal Bagh.

Banerghatta National Park

Lal Bagh, Mavalli, Bengaluru;
Entry Fee: *Adults: ₹10, Children: Free;*
Car parking: *₹10;* **Timings**: *6 a.m.–7 p.m.*

The lush green Cubbon Park in Bengaluru is a popular haunt of both locals and tourists

Statues of Queen Victoria and King Edward, gazebos to rest tired legs, thickets of bamboo, neat grassy stretches, a tennis academy, a children's park and rocky outcrops are housed inside the 300 acres of Cubbon Park (erstwhile Meade's Park). The green fold of the park also houses three major monuments of the city: the Seshadri Iyer Memorial Library, the 1876-built State Archaeological Museum and the Attara Kacheri (court). There is no traffic between 5–8 a.m. for the convenience of walkers. The park closes at 8 p.m. in the evening. A much-needed respite from the swarm of traffic around it, these parks are the lungs of Bengaluru.

Dodda Basavanagudi (Bull Temple) and Ganesha Temple

One of the most popular sightseeing spots of the city, the Bull Temple stays with one as an endearing image of Bengaluru. Built in 1537, this

Nandi at Dodda Basavanagudi

temple is dedicated to Shiva's *vahana* (vehicle), Nandi. A large rocky outcrop, known as Bugle Rock, straddles the temple compound as you walk towards the right from the adjacent Ganesha temple. The towering Nandi statue of 15 feet is said to be one of the biggest in India.

Basavanagudi, Bengaluru;
Timings: *7.30 a.m.–8.30 p.m.*

Tipu Sultan's Fort

Remnants of Tipu's rule are aplenty in and around Bengaluru. Tipu's Fort in Bengaluru sits at the far end of a well-manicured garden. It is the deceptively double-storeyed and rather inornate structure that made for the summer palace of Tipu Sultan (1781). Not in sync with the modern development around it, the fort sits like an oasis in-between newly constructed buildings. The characteristic Indo-Islamic architectural features, wooden pillars and the unexpectedly cool flooring (even on a hot day) on the ground floor are the highlights.

Albert Victor Road, Chamrajpet, Bengaluru;
Ph: 080-26706836; **Entry Fee**: *Indians: ₹5, Foreigners: ₹100;* **Video**: *₹25;*
Timings: *8.30 a.m.–5.30 p.m.*

Bangalore Fort

Evading the modern tourists' itinerary, the elusive Bangalore Fort is a starkly peaceful haven and critical historical slice of Bengaluru as compared to the bustling KR Market outside. This is the only remaining part of the original fort built by Kempe Gowda in AD 1537,

The Bangalore Fort, which was built by Kempe Gowda and expanded by Tipu Sultan

A trip to Malleshwaram orients tourists to the oldest temples in the city

which later changed hands to Hyder Ali and then Lord Cornwallis. In fact, a tablet in the wall is a testimony that this is where Lord Cornwallis took possession of the fort in AD 1791. The fort now houses a Ganesha temple, three gateways and a dungeon, which is closed for visitors.

KR Market, Bengaluru;
Timings: *9 a.m.–5.30 p.m.*

Temple Street, Malleshwaram

The decidedly Hindu part of the town, Malleshwaram is perfect for a temple fix for both pilgrims and tourists. Here, Kadu Malleshwara, Nandeeshwara, Lakshmi Narsimha and the Gangamma Devi temples sit close by. The grandest of the four is the Kadu Malleshwara Temple. True to its name, the Shiva temple lies in a thicket of greens – *kadu* means forest in Kannada. Its tranquil environment is an alluring backdrop for meditation and yoga. On the opposite side of the road, Nandeeshwara's legacy goes back 7,000 years ago; the temple was excavated much later from beneath layers of soil. It also has a *kalyani* inside (a stepped temple pond). Gangamma Temple and Lakshmi Narsimha lie adjacent to Kadu Malleshwara, and are usually bursting at the seams with morning worshippers.

Basavanagudi, Bengaluru; **Timings**: *7.30 a.m.–Noon, 5 p.m.–8.30 p.m.*

Venkatappa Art Gallery and Government Museum

Vintage artefacts, weathered utility objects, weapons, musical instruments and paintings sprawl all over the double-storeyed halls of Bengaluru's museum. Only a few references to the sixteenth-century king, Tipu Sultan, draws an interest to the otherwise tawdry presentation. Despite insufficient information or guides, this seems to be a favourite with schools. Avoid weekends when schools bring in hoards of children. The attached Venkatappa Gallery is a slight relief with well-displayed sculptures dating back to second century AD.

Kasturba Road, Bengaluru;
Ph: 080-22864483; **Entry Fee**: *Adults: ₹4, Children: ₹2;* **Timings**: *10 a.m.–5 p.m.*

HAL Heritage Centre and Aerospace Museum

A low-key complex, the HAL Heritage Centre and Aerospace Museum is home to six decades of aviation history of India. The neat exhibits and photographs of the Hindustan Aeronautics Limited (HAL) Museum affirm Bengaluru's importance as the City of Aeronautics. The models of early planes and helicopters used by the Indian aviation industry are an interesting infusion to the experience. In fact, one can also climb to the Heritage Centre ATC to view the runway of the old airport.

Old Airport Road, Bengaluru;
Ph: 080-25228341; www.hal-india.com;
Entry Fee: *₹30;* **Camera**: *₹50;*
Timings: *9 a.m.–5 p.m.*

St Mary's Basilica

Wedged in the middle of the thickly populated Shivaji Nagar, the white

St Mary's Basilica is the oldest church in Bengaluru

steeple of St Mary's Basilica can be seen piercing the sky from afar. The basilica has watched over the area since the seventeenth century and requires only a quick stop while exploring the Commercial Street–Shivaji Nagar area.

Shivaji Nagar, Bengaluru;
Ph: 080-22865434; www.stmarybasilica.in;
Timings: *5 a.m.–10 p.m.*

Wonder La

If you are travelling with kids, this is an imperative addition to your trip. Wonder La has fifty state-of-the-art land and water rides, and is one of the best amusement parks in the city. These are divided into Kids, Water, Dry and High Thrill! Keep a full day at hand, as it will be impossible to tear your kids away from this place. Carry a change of clothes and (own) towels when visiting here. Wonder La also has an in-house luxury resort for overnight guests.

Mysore Road, Ph: 080-22010333; www.wonderla.com; **Entry Fee:** *Adults: ₹640, Children: ₹500 (Weekday); Adults: ₹800, Children: ₹590 (Weekend & public holidays);* **Fast Track Tickets:** *Adults: ₹1,280, Children: ₹1,000 (Weekday); Adults: ₹1,600, Children: ₹1,180 (Weekend & public holidays); Peak season rates are higher;* **Timings:** *Mon–Fri: 11 a.m.–6 p.m., Sat-Sun: 11 a.m.–7 p.m.*

Jawaharlal Nehru Planetarium

If travelling with kids, the planetarium and science park is a great addition to your itinerary. Founded in 1989, the well-maintained thirty science exhibits and regular shows for 45 minutes can be seen in the spacious campus in the middle of the city. A new show, 'Dawn of the Space Age', has been recently launched and starts at 1.30 p.m.

Sri T Chowdaiah Road, High Grounds, Bengaluru; Ph: 080-22379725; www.taralaya.org; **Entry Fee:** *Adults: ₹30, Children: ₹20;* **Show Timings in English:** *12.30 p.m., 1.30 p.m., 4.30 p.m., 5.30 p.m. Closed on Mondays and second Tuesdays.*

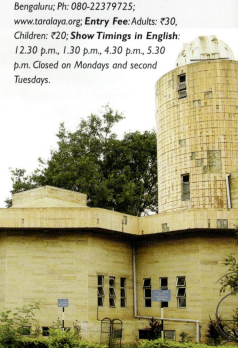

The Nehru Planetarium in Bengaluru

Experience Karnataka

ACCOMMODATION

Bengaluru's hospitality scape encompasses a vast variety of options from hotels, guesthouses, business hotels and homestays.

CASA COTTAGE

Tucked away in the narrow green streets of centrally located Richmond Town, Casa Cottage's legacy of almost a century is still intact in its vintage look, period furniture and soothing ambience. The first-floor rooms are more spacious and have a private sit-out that overlooks a grassy patch in front. The café by the garden serves only breakfast. Casa Cottage hits the perfect price point for tourists looking for a heritage experience, coupled with personalized service, in the heart of the town.

2, Clapham Street, Richmond Town (Behind Richmond Town Post Office), Bengaluru; Ph: 080-22990337; www.casacottage.com;
Tariff: ₹4,000–5,500 plus taxes.

THE CHANCERY PAVILION

The Chancery Pavilion makes a good choice for tourists who are looking to stay at the centre of the city with all the comforts of a high-end hotel at a reasonable price. Since the hotel offers the best available rate, you can get a great deal at the last minute. The hotel offers facilities like Wi-fi, swimming pool and multi-cuisine restaurants – Ithaca, Indian Affair – as well as Amnesia, the lounge bar.

135, Residency Road, Bengaluru;
Ph: 080-41414141; www.chanceryhotels.com;
Tariff: ₹5,047–61,555 plus taxes.

ESCAPE AN URBAN RESERVE

Inspired by the world's most stylish cities (New York, London and Tokyo), the thirty-roomed boutique hotel on 100 Feet Road is fashioned in a contemporary mood, with relaxing interiors. One can look forward to personalized service with modern amenities like a rooftop pool, Wi-fi, well-equipped spa and a gym. Its restaurant Bricklane Grill offers a wide range of multi-cuisine dishes. Ask for the Executive Room with a terrace deck if you want a breezy private sit-out to enjoy the Bengaluru weather. Centrally located, it is close to the city's favourite shopping destinations, business centres and dining options.

770, 100 Feet Road, Indiranagar, Bengaluru;
Ph: 080-42415555; www.escapehotels.in;
Tariff: ₹4,750–5,250 plus taxes.

GRAND MERCURE BANGALORE

Photographs of Hampi lead you through the corridors and rooms of Mercure, as the mood of the hotel slowly shifts from heritage to contemporary and chic. A poolside café, gym, spa, a deli, Wi-fi facilities and cycles to hire make the stay at Mercure comfortable and full of activities to fill your day. When choosing rooms from the studio to large suites, ensure that you book as per your group size as the single suite can be pretty snug. While the 12th Main offers global cuisine, By The Blue offers Indian cuisine and grills.

12th Main, 3rd Block, Koramangala, Bengaluru;
Ph: 080-45121212; www.grandmercurebangalore.com;
Tariff: ₹11,037–11,667 plus taxes.

ITC GARDENIA

Immersed in green, ITC's Gardenia is eco-inclined and stands for responsible luxury. Excellent hospitality, uniquely themed rooms, a helipad, Wi-fi, pool, six dining options and a list of awards and accolades behind it, this one cannot disappoint you. Cubbon Pavilion, the multi-cuisine restaurant is open 24 hours. Its other restaurants, Lotus Pavilion, K&K, Edo, Ottimo and the bar Highland Nectar are great places for a meal and to unwind.

1, Residency Road, Bengaluru;
Ph: 080-40580444; www.itchotels.in;
Tariff: ₹11,500 onwards plus taxes.

JAYAMAHAL PALACE
Wooden floors creaking below the carpets, high ceilings and the spacious rooms of Jayamahal Palace are reminiscent of the old colonial architecture and the grandeur of the 19-acre property of the Raja of Gondal. This heritage hotel has an aged vibe but is fitted with facilities like a swimming pool, Wi-fi zone, multi-cuisine bar and restaurants. The standard rooms in the non-heritage wing of the hotel are ideal for the price conscious. Gallops offers multi-cuisine dishes and its other restaurant, Golden, serves global cuisine.
1, Jayamahal Road, Bengaluru; Ph: 080-40580444; www.jayamahalpalace.in; Tariff: ₹2,975–7,525 plus taxes.

JÜSTA HOTELS & RESORTS
Tagore's Shantiniketan now lives on MG Road at the jüSTa Hotels & Resorts, in the form of handpicked canvasses of students from the art school. This boutique hotel of 18 rooms at a central, yet secluded, location is a perfect choice over its five-star neighbours. It also offers a travel desk, pick-up service (from the airport or station), free Wi-fi, and prompt and pleasant service to go with it. Its rooftop multi-cuisine restaurant serves Indian, Chinese, and Continental fare.
- jüSTa MG Road, 21/14, Craig Park Layout, MG Road, Bengaluru; Ph: 080-41135555; Tariff (incl. breakfast, excl. taxes): ₹4,222–5,958.
- jüSTa Off MG Road, 30/1, 2nd Cross, Ulsoor Road, Ulsoor, Bengaluru; Ph: 080-41134488; Tariff (incl. breakfast, excl. taxes): ₹4,222.
- jüSTa Indiranagar, 796, 1st Cross, 12th Main, HAL 2nd Stage, Indiranagar, Bengaluru; Ph: 080-42044040; www.justahotels.com; Tariff (incl. breakfast, excl. taxes): ₹4,222.

THE LEELA PALACE
High-end facilities, aesthetic Indian interiors and rich ambience of one of the poshest addresses in town translate into the luxurious Leela Palace Hotel. The dull pink architecture of the hotel has been inspired from the royal splendour of Mysuru. More than four dining options (Jamavar, Citrus, Zen, Le Cirque Signature, The Cake Shop), a bar (The Library Bar), swimming pool, spa, Wi-fi and a shopping arcade are available for guests.
23, Kodihalli, Old Airport Road, Bengaluru; Ph: 080-25211234; www.theleela.com; Tariff: ₹11,250–26,000 plus taxes.

OLDE BANGALORE
Recreating the old-world charm of Bengaluru, right from the untreated bricks made from earth to the canteen where all staff and management eat together and from the South Parade restaurant to the large gulmohar tree in the courtyard, Olde Bangalore is a retreat in Devanhalli (en route to the airport). You could also eat at the coffee shop, By/Two, and pick up a baked item or two from its bakery, Muffins. If someone had made the effort to plant a gulmohar tree in a courtyard to recreate an MG Road experience, this was surely going to be different. Also, the fact that it's just 30km (1 hour from MG Road) away from the city makes it an ideal choice for those who want some respite from the hustle and bustle of city life.
206, Utopia, Tarabanahalli, Chikkajala, Bengaluru; Ph: 080-28010100; www.oldebangalore.in; Tariff: Approx. ₹7,000 plus taxes.

PURPLE LOTUS
Just off St Marks Road near MG Road, Purple Lotus' decor is minimalistic and refreshing. True to its name, the boutique hotel is dotted with lotus ponds and lotus-themed stone art. The simple yet tasteful interiors of the rooms is infused with indoor plants to add a dash of green. The hotel also has a yoga studio and spa, along with Wi-fi facilities and a business centre. Its in-house restaurant, Lotus Café, too is neatly done. What's most interesting is that the site of the hotel was once home to freedom fighter,

Experience Karnataka

Hon. Sri MV Krishnappa.
46, 6th Cross, Lavelle Road, Bengaluru;
Ph: 080-40056300; www.purplelotus.in;
Tariff: ₹9,000–9,950 plus taxes.

THE RITZ-CARLTON
Notching up the hospitality scape of Bengaluru, The Ritz-Carlton is an escape to serenity. Indulge in the property's excellent rooms, central location, several dining options and slight nuances of luxury in every aspect of the experience.
99, Residency Road, Shanthala Nagar, Ashok Nagar, Bengaluru; Ph: 080-49148000; www.ritzcarlton.com;
Tariff: ₹15,900–37,000 plus taxes.

VILLA CAMELOT
A B&B, the sunny hospitality of Raghu and Yamini is the highlight of the stay at Villa Camelot, while you share stories over delicious home-made food, enjoy the open spaces of the modern house and the couple's love for movies, music and Bengaluru. All the rooms are Indian themed, aesthetically pleasant with toiletries and snacks thrown in as part of the package. The 'Mogra' set of rooms on the ground floor are suitable for large families or long-stay guests who would like to have a kitchenette at hand. Though the 'Krishnaa' room on the second floor is the most comfy with air conditioning and a personal sit-out. This is ideal for long-stay guests who have work in Whitefield.
94/95, 4th Cross, ECC Road, Prithvi Layout, Whitefield, Bengaluru; Ph: 080-32723965; Tariff: On request.

VILLA POTTIPATI
Another heritage secret, Villa Pottipati (now run by the Neemrana Hotels group) lures you to its classic charm with black and white pictures on the walls, weathered antiques and period furniture. Named after the village of the Reddy family that owned it, the five rooms and three suites of the ochre-walled garden home are named after traditional saris of south India. A heady aroma of seasonal fruits and flowers hangs in the lush garden.
142, 8th Cross, 4th Main, Malleshwaram, Bengaluru;
Ph: 080-23360777; www.neemranahotels.com;
Tariff: ₹4,000–5,500 plus taxes.

VIVANTA – BY TAJ
Vivanta – By Taj stands at the end of the arterial MG Road and offers its signature five-star luxury by way of contemporary decor in its rooms, superior hospitality and amenities like a swimming pool and Wi-fi. The highlights of the hotel include guided heritage walks of Bengaluru, Sous Vide Culinary Art (a style of cooking at Graze, the in-house restaurant) and pampering your senses with customized gourmet menu.
■ 41/3, MG Road, Bengaluru;
Ph: 080-66604444; www.vivantabytaj.com; Tariff (incl. breakfast, excl. taxes): ₹17,250 onwards.
■ 2275, Tumkur Road, Yeshwantpur, Bengaluru;
Ph: 080-66900111; Tariff (incl. breakfast, excl. taxes): ₹6,500 onwards.
■ ITPB, Whitefield, Bengaluru;
Ph: 080-6693 3333; Tariff (incl. breakfast, excl. taxes): ₹6,500 onwards.

EATING OUT

With new eateries popping up every other week, the ever-changing food scene of Bengaluru is one that is difficult to keep pace with. But that also means that there are immense options and variety for tourists to satiate both their hunger pangs as well as cravings for any kind of cuisine.

100 FT.

Bengaluru's first boutique restaurant and namesake to the most popular high street of the city, the white, soothing ambience transports one to a Mediterranean village. Simple and brilliantly cooked food and excellent service makes 100 ft. one of those places where you can never go wrong. With 12 years of experience behind them, they have perfected favourites like 'Tian of vegetables' and the grills.
777/i, 100 Feet Road, HAL 2nd Stage, Indiranagar, Bengaluru; Ph: 080-25277752; www.100ft.in; Timings: 11 a.m.–11 p.m.; Meal for 2: ₹1,000 onwards.

BRICKLANE GRILL

An elaborate Parsi menu along with additional Indian and Continental cuisines at the fifth floor, the all-white, partially open-air Bricklane Grill is luring enough to bring you to the restaurant time and again. You can also choose to sit in a private room or the seating area that overlooks the pool, where the aroma from the live counter fills the air.
770, 100 Feet Road, Indiranagar, Bengaluru; Ph: 080-42415505; www.escapehotels.in; Timings: 7 a.m.–11.30 p.m.; Meal for 2: ₹1,000 onwards.

THE BLACK RABBIT

New on the block, The Black Rabbit's pleasant interiors, excellent service and delicious Continental food is making the restaurant one of the favourites in the city. It lies on 100 Feet Road, making it easily accessible.
770, 100 Feet Road, Indiranagar, Bengaluru; Ph: 080-42415575; Timings: Noon–11.30 p.m.; Meal for 2: ₹1,000 onwards.

COORG

A 'weekend only' special, Priya and KC Aiyappa's Coorgi food will keep you dreaming the whole week for the authentic home-made food! Traditional techniques, personally treated meats and fresh spices are the highlights of the food. The rooftop buffet place is bustling with regulars, so book ahead for weekend lunch here.
477, Krishna Temple Road, 1st Stage, Indiranagar, Bengaluru; Ph: 09845493688; Timings: Fri: 8–11 p.m., Sat-Sun: Noon–3.30 p.m., 8–11 p.m.; Meal for 2: ₹500–750.

EBONY

Enjoy the spectacular panoramic view of the cityscape from the 13th floor, along with a substantial multi-cuisine menu. Daily lunches are Indian buffet with a less-than-robust salad selection compensated by delicious Biryani (rice dish). Dinner is served à la carte. The view from Ebony is the best thing on the menu.
Hotel Ivory Tower, The Penthouse Floor, Barton Centre, 84, MG Road, Bengaluru; Ph: 080-41311101; www.ebonywithaview.com; Timings: 12.30–3 p.m., 7.30–11 p.m.; Meal for 2: ₹750–1,000.

EMPIRE

Post-pub-hopping hunger pangs bring hundreds to the 14 Empire restaurants in and around the city (the flagship one being on Church Street) in the after-hours of Bengaluru. Prepare to bag the first seat that you get and order from the most popular Coin Parotta, Ghee Rice, Chicken Kebab and other Indian and Chinese dishes.
36, Church Street Road, Bengaluru; Ph: 080-40414041; www.hotelempire.in; Timings: 10.30 a.m.–12.30 a.m.; Meal for 2: ₹500–750.

Experience Karnataka

THE FATTY BAO
Step in at the Fatty Bao to surprise your taste buds with a twist to the usual Asian fare. From the house of Monkey Bar, the restaurant's baos cannot be missed.
610, 3rd Floor, 12th-A, Main Road, Off 80 Feet Road, HAL 2nd Stage, Indiranagar, Bengaluru; Ph: 080-44114499; Timings: Noon–11.30 p.m.; Meal for 2: ₹1,000 onwards.

HALLI MANE
The mud-plastered walls and hand-painted traditional designs, Carnatic music and traditionally dressed waiters are in sync with the typical south Indian rural fare (think Ragi Mudde, Kundapura Pathrode and Akki Rotti) that is served here. A ₹150-coupon gets you an elaborate lunch which cannot be shared; else you can choose to eat at the ground-floor, self-service section.
3rd Cross, Sampige Road, Malleshwaram, Bengaluru; Ph: 080-65611222; www.hallimane.com; Timings: Noon–3.30 p.m., 7–11.30 p.m.; Meal for 2: ₹250–500.

IMLI
The bright-yellow cheerful walls of Imli and the airy seating on the first floor add to the excellent north Indian fare with specials like Khichdi aur Baingan Bhaaja, Maa ki Dal and Moong Dal ka Chilla. Though packed during meals, you can enjoy a glass of *chai* and some fresh *chaat* over a host of board games in the early evening.
204, 5th Main, 7th Cross, Indiranagar 1st Stage, Bengaluru; Ph: 080-40949464; www.imli.co.in; Timings: 11 a.m.–11 p.m; Meal for 2: ₹500–750.

KONARK
An ideal choice for vegetarians, Konark's central location near MG Road, excellent quality of food, family appropriate ambience and prompt service has helped it stay on the top of the list for years.
50, Field Marshall Cariappa Road, Residency Road, Bengaluru; Ph: 080-41248812; Timings: 8 a.m.–10.30 p.m.; Meal for 2: ₹250–500.

KOSHYS
This hallmark hangout for authors, artistes, actors and disoriented foreign tourists trying to make sense of the elaborate menu, stands as the bastion of old Bengaluru. Past clientele include Jawaharlal Nehru and the Queen of England. Uniformed waiters walk around busily with steel trays, balancing favourites like Mutton Cutlets, Potato Smileys, Baked Beans, pots of tea and Caramel Custard.
39, St Marks Road, Bengaluru; Ph: 080-22213793; Timings: 9 a.m.–11 p.m.; Meal for 2: ₹500–750.

MANGALORE PEARL
A veritable option for coastal Kannada cuisine, Mangalore Pearl offers Karnataka-themed graffiti on all the walls by famous cartoonist, Prakash Shetty, along with favourites like Sol Kadi (a delicious concoction of kokum and curd but looks like a strawberry milkshake) and prawns.
3, Coles Road, Above KC Das Sweets, Frazer Town, Bengaluru; Ph: 080-25578855; www.mangalorepearl.com; Timings: Noon–2.45 p.m., 7.30–10.30 p.m.; Meal for 2: ₹500–700.

MONKEY BAR
The easy-going vibe of Monkey Bar immediately kicks in a good mood! Distressed walls, a vintage Lambretta scooter, quirky posters and an equally fun menu to choose from, makes this an all-day favourite. Given the young ambience of the bar, it's no wonder that dishes like Butterfly Chicken 'Gangnam Style' have found their way into the menu. Don't miss the burgers!
610, 12th Main, Indiranagar, Towards 80 Feet Road, Opp. SBI, Bengaluru; Ph: 080-44114455; www.mobar.in; Timings: Noon–11.30 p.m.; Meal for 2: ₹1,000 onwards.

OLIVE BAR & KITCHEN
Decidedly Mediterranean with its white-blue ambience and cuisine, the Olive Bar & Kitchen exudes exclusivity. The extensive variety of

drinks and food are perfect for a long Sunday brunch.
16, Wood Street, Ashok Nagar, Bengaluru; Ph: 080-41128400; www.olivebarandkitchen.com; Timings: Noon–11.30 p.m.; Meal for 2: ₹1,000 onwards.

PHOBIDDEN FRUIT
Phobidden Fruit hits the nail on the head with a perfect, cosy ambience and refreshing Vietnamese cuisine. Try the typical rice noodle soup, Pho, for an authentic Oriental infusion to your meal.
12th Main Road, Domlur, Indiranagar, Bengaluru; Ph: 080-41255175; Timings: Noon–3.30 p.m., 7–11 p.m.; Meal for 2: ₹500–750.

PUJA RESTAURANT AT AJANTHA HOTEL
Almost five decades old, Puja Restaurant is where you can get your dose of a full south Indian meal. Dollops of rice, Rasam, Upp Saaru and Avare Kal complemented by a sweet and pickles make the thali. The centrally located Puja makes for a great lunch stop if you are hanging around MG Road.
22-A, Mahatma Gandhi Road, Bengaluru; Ph: 080-25584321; www.hotelajatha.in; Timings: Noon–3.30 p.m., 7–11.30 p.m.; Meal for 2: ₹250–500.

RED FORK DELI
The Dhansak, Chicken Farcha and Lagan-nu-Custard never disappoint at Red Fork Deli in Indiranagar. Step in for authentic Parsi food, served with a heavy dose of warm personal touch.
594, 12th Main Road, HAL 2nd Stage, Indiranagar, Bengaluru; Ph: 080-41154372; www.daddysdeli.in; Timings: 9 a.m.–10.30 p.m.; Meal for 2: ₹500–750.

SAVOURY RESTAURANT
You know you are in the IT capital of India, if a restaurant serves 'Internet' and 'Computer' Arabian milkshake. This apart, Savoury Restaurant is famous for its shawarmas.
56, Mosque Road, Frazer Town, Bengaluru; Timings: 8.30 a.m.–11 p.m.; Meal for 2: ₹250–750.

SECRET GARDEN
This elusive rooftop restaurant is made for a long hearty lunch of home-made salads, soups and sinful desserts. A blackboard menu and an open kitchen add to the intimacy of Secret Garden.
7/1, Edward Road, Off Queens Road, Bengaluru; Ph: 080-41131365; Timings: Noon–4 p.m. (Sundays closed); Meal for 2: ₹750–1,000.

SMOKE HOUSE DELI
Hand-painted graffiti adorns the bright white walls of Smoke House Deli. Be pleasantly surprised with detailed explanations about the ingredients and method of making a dish by the waiting staff. If nothing else, you will leave more knowledgeable.
1209, Ward No. 72, Domlur, HAL 2nd Stage, 100 Feet Road, Indiranagar, Bengaluru; Ph: 080-25200898; www.smokehousedeli.in; Timings: 9 a.m.–11 p.m.; Meal for 2: ₹1,000 onwards.

SOO RA SANG
Surprise your taste buds with Oriental cooking at the authentic Korean restaurant run by Yung. Traditional Korean seating, barbecue special tables, cold Cinnamon Tea after a meal and excellent food with a helping hand if you need recommendations.
Sapathagiri Pride, 697, 6th Cross, HAL 3rd Stage, Kodihalli, Bengaluru; Ph: 080-41303435; Timings: Noon–11 p.m.; Meal for 2: ₹500–750.

SRI KRISHNA CAFÉ
For a stomach-stretching Tamil-style lunch, there is nothing more worth your while than Sri Krishna Café. Do not expect much from the ambience, and concentrate on ordering from a variety of idlis, puris, vadas, uthappams, idiyappams, meals, etc.
143, KHB Colony, 1st Floor, 60 Feet Road, 5th Block,

Experience Karnataka

Koramangala, Bengaluru; Ph: 080-41104345; Timings: 7.30–11 a.m., Noon–3.30 p.m., 5.30–10.30 p.m.; Meal for 2: ₹250–500.

SUNNY'S
Named after a Golden Retriever, Sunny's is a great pick for the best gourmet Italian and European cuisine in town. The wood-fire, thin-crust pizzas are a favourite with regulars.
34, Embassy Diamante, Vittal Mallya Road, Opp. Canara Bank, Bengaluru; Ph: 080-41329391; www.sunnysbangalore.in; Timings: Noon–3.30 p.m., 7–11 p.m.; Meal for 2: ₹1,000 onwards.

URBAN SOLACE
Urban Solace's tag line reads 'café for the soul'. This explains why it is one of the favourite lake-facing cafés of Bengaluru. After all, no other place gives you the luxury of sipping wine with a brilliant view of the Ulsoor waters. The café packs in a variety of combos and weekend specials along with literary, stand-up comedy and musical events on different days of the week.

2, Annaswamy Mudaliar Road, Bengaluru; Ph: 080-25553656; www.urbansolace.biz; Timings: 11 a.m.–11 p.m., Sat-Sun: 8 a.m.–11 p.m.; Meal for 2: ₹250–500.

VIDYARTHI BHAVAN
Vidyarthi Bhavan is a time-tested Bengaluru joint, serving south Indian tiffin items and meals since 1943. Old-world ambience and crispy dosas served by waiters in traditional *dhotis* is an additional highlight of the restaurant.
32, Gandhi Bazaar Main Road, Basavanagudi, Bengaluru; Ph: 080-26677588; Timings: Mon–Thurs: 6.30–11.30 a.m., 2–8 p.m., Sat-Sun/Govt. Holidays: 6.30 a.m.–Noon, 2.30–8 p.m., Fridays closed; Meal for 2: ₹250 onwards.

DESSERTS

CORNER HOUSE
One of the oldest dessert joints of the city, Corner House has been dishing out the best ice-cream combos for over 25 years. The popularity of

STREET FOOD: THINDI BEEDI

Eat Street (officially Old Market Road) stretches for 500 metres and starts stirring with activity at 6.30 p.m. The otherwise lazy street transforms into a bustling mass of people hollering for their *chaat* orders, local snacks, juice, paper dosas and sweets. The crowd really swells after 8 p.m. and is abuzz with foodies until 11 p.m. Try local Kannada favourites like milk-dipping Chirotti and flavours from other parts of India.
VV Puram, Bengaluru; Timings: 6.30–11.30 p.m.

favourites like Death by Chocolate, seasonal fruit and ice-cream combos and the classic Hot Chocolate Fudge prompted the chain to open 15 outlets in Bengaluru and one in Mysuru.
45/3, Gopalkrishna Complex, Near Mayo Hall, Residency Road, Bengaluru; Ph: 080-25583262; www.cornerhouse.in; Timings: 11 a.m.–11.30 p.m.; Meal for 2: ₹250–500.

NASI AND MEE
Relatively new on the block, Nasi and Mee offers a simple menu and then lives up to it. The restaurant has managed to attract quite a following in a short span of time. This is Koramangala's new hotspot — one that should not be missed by anyone who has a palate for authentic Asian food.
974, 4th Cross, 80 Feet Main Road, 4th Block, Koramangala, Bengaluru; Ph: 080-41513456; Timings: 12.30–3.30 p.m., 7–11 p.m.; Meal for 2: ₹500–750.

SPOONFUL OF SUGAR
This cosy little café at Indiranagar packs in scrumptious desserts with large helpings that could be an entire meal by itself. The Banoffee Pie and Blueberry Cheesecake are particularly popular. One can also get some insider tips with a baking workshop with Sangeeta and Yuvna, the mother–daughter duo who own this blissful sweet-treat for Bangaloreans.
421g, 1st Main, 3rd Cross, 1st Stage, Indiranagar, Bengaluru; Ph: 080-25255534; Timings: 10.30 a.m.–8.30 p.m.; Meal for 2: ₹500–750.

BREAKFAST SPECIALS

AIRLINES
Early morning joggers, students and old-timers make the quorum under the shade of two large Banyan trees at Airlines. Do not expect prompt service, but do look out for delicious south Indian tiffin items. A breakfast of Shivage Bhath, idlis and dosas is recommended to be washed down with coffee! In fact, if you are feeling lazy to step out of your car, there is a drive-in service as well.
4, Madras Bank Road, Off Lavelle Road, Bengaluru; Ph: 080-22273783; Timings: 7 a.m.–10 p.m.; Meal for 2: ₹250.

THE HOLE IN THE WALL
The best hangover remedies are packed in juicy sausages, veggies and eggs complemented by fresh juices at The Hole in the Wall. This is one breakfast place that you don't want to miss.
4, 8th Main, Koramangala 4th Block, Bengaluru; Ph: 080-40949490; Timings: Tue–Fri: 8 a.m.–3 p.m., 5.30–8.30 p.m., Sat-Sun: 8 a.m.–3 p.m., Mondays closed; Meal for 2: ₹250–500.

MAVALLI TIFFIN ROOM (MTR)
Old Bengaluru nostalgia, served with authentic south Indian food can only be sampled at MTR on Lal Bagh Road. The pure-veg delights are served in silver if you are going with Bangalore Walks and if you are on your own, you might need to jostle for some space and share the table with strangers. Nevertheless, the experience is enriching.
14, Lal Bagh Road, Bengaluru; Ph: 080-22230471; Timings: 6.30 a.m.–11 p.m., 12.30–2 p.m., 3.30–8.30 p.m., Mondays closed; Dinner: 7.45–9 p.m. only on Sat-Sun; Meal for 2: ₹250.

TAAZA THINDI
Immaculately clean, optimally priced, and delicious food make Taaza Thindi swarm with breakfast goers in Jayanagar's 4th Block. The restaurant believes in keeping it simple but delivering excellent food.
26th Main, 4th Block, Jayanagar, Bengaluru; Ph: 07676208899; Timings: 7 a.m.–Noon, 4.30–9.30 p.m.; Meal for 2: ₹250.

CAFÉS

BRAHMIN'S CAFÉ
Hinged on its nostalgic value, the popularity of the spartan menu of six items since 1945 (Idli,

Experience Karnataka

Vada, Khara Bhath, Kesari Bhath, Badam Milk and coffee) is still intact with regulars.
3, Ranga Rao Road, Shankarapuram, Bengaluru; Timings: 6 a.m.–Noon, 3–7 p.m., Sundays closed; Meal for 2: ₹250.

CAFÉ MAX
German and European cuisines plus the great Bengaluru weather is why you will find the rooftop Café Max buzzing with people. You can add wine to accompany the food and end it with sinful desserts. If you are just there for coffee, we doubt you will leave without asking about the soft yummy cookie that comes with it.
716, CMH Road, 3rd Floor, Rooftop of Goethe Institute/Max Mueller Bhavan, Indiranagar, Bengaluru; Ph: 080-41200469; www.cafe-max.in; Timings: Weekdays: 11 a.m.–11 p.m., Weekends: 10 a.m.–11 p.m.; Meal for 2: ₹500–750.

INDIAN COFFEE HOUSE
Legendary visitors of the café include artistes, freedom fighters and *jhola*-wielding intellectuals. For a nostalgic trip, go to Indian Coffee House where turbaned waiters hastily push the spartan menu in front of you. Take in the aged vibe of crumbling walls, old coffee posters, unpretentious furniture and the constant chatter with some rose milk and cutlets.
Ground Floor, Coffee House, 19, Church Street, Brigade Gardens, Bengaluru; Ph: 080-25587088; Timings: 8 a.m.–8.30 p.m.; Meal for 2: ₹250.

INFINITEA
A tea room ambience meets you in a warm atmosphere with photographs and wood furniture at Infinitea. The menu is large enough to choose an entire meal or just a quick cup of tea and dessert.
2, Shah Sultan Complex, Cunningham Road, Bengaluru; Ph: 080-41148428; Timings: 11 a.m.–11 p.m.; Meal for 2: ₹250.

LAKE VIEW
Started in 1930 by James Meadow Charles, Lake View is one of the oldest establishments on MG Road. It changed hands in 1947 to Vraj Lal. The legendary Black Forest Cake is what brings people here.
89, Kanan Bldg., MG Road, Bengaluru; Ph: 080-25582161; www.lakeviewmilkbar.com; Timings: 8.30 a.m.–Midnight; Meal for 2: ₹250.

OM MADE CAFÉ
Ideal for a sunset view on a breezy Bengaluru evening, pair the vistas with your choice of wine at Om Made Café in Koramangala. Flat Bread, Croque Monsieur and Chicken Wrap are good picks from the menu.
136, Above Gold's Gym, 1st Cross, 5th Block, Koramangala, Bengaluru; Timings: Noon–11 p.m.; Meal for 2: ₹750–1,000.

WHERE TO GO PUB HOPPING

The beer bastion of the country, Bengaluru doesn't disappoint with its rock music backdrop to easy-going pubs. Here are the top picks.

ARBOR BREWING COMPANY

Arbor Brewing Company promises to make you more brew savvy. Seven special brews and more to come are the highlight of this American-styled, spacious minimalistic brewery! The menu suggests the best pub fare that goes with the different ales along with a short history of how it came to be!
Magrath Road, Bengaluru; Ph: 080-50144477; www.arborbrewing.in

LOCAL

A brick-walled, open-air, beer-serving place makes for the perfect recipe for an ideal Bengaluru evening. A 'terrace drinkery' as the signage claims, this Koramangala joint is one of the best places to grab a cold one and hum along to the 'all familiar' soft and alternative rock music.
467, Terrace Floor, Above Jimi's, 80 Feet Road, 6th Block, Koramangala, Bengaluru; Ph: 080-25505119; www.thelocaldrinkery.com

OPUS

The Goan-themed watering hole and live-gigs venue, with a charming octopus as a mascot, is a favourite with karaoke singers. The designated karaoke nights raise up the action – we assure you will leave after making new friends.
4, 1st Main, Chakravarthy Layout, Palace Cross Road, Bengaluru; Ph: 09844030198; www.myopus.in; Timings: 11.30 a.m.–11.30 p.m.

TOIT

Bengaluru's redemption from a dwindling pub culture came in 2010, with Toit's non-establishment, largish, wooden-floored brewery, which can fit about 400 beer drinkers at a point of time. Inspired by Pepé Le Pew (the skunk of the Looney Tunes fame), find the mascot lounging on the logo which announces Toit to be 'sending it since 2010' (a true-blue Bangalorean phrase for downing drinks). Pets are allowed in one section.
298, 100 Feet Road, Metro Pillar 62, Indiranagar, Bengaluru; Ph: 080-25201460; www.toit.in; Timings: 11 a.m.–11 p.m.

WATSONS

Overlooking a vast sprawl of green treetops, Watsons has hit the chord with beer lovers and those who thrive in semi-open-air pubs. The music and energy revvs up slowly through the evening and reaches a crescendo when the pub is about to close. Its semi-open-air space and the view of the lush Ulsoor area are the highlights.
974, Skywalk, 4th Floor, Near Body Craft, Assaye Road, Ulsoor, Bengaluru; Ph: 07760988933; Timings: 11 a.m.–11 p.m.

WINDMILLS CRAFTWORKS

The book-lined walls and perfect acoustics around a small stage for live gigs adds to the open-air wooden deck of Windmills in Whitefield. The six in-house brews and largely American cuisine can be ordered innovatively on a tablet.
331, Road 5B, EPIP Zone, Whitefield, Bengaluru; Ph: 080-25692012; www.windmillscraftworks.com; Timings: 12.30–3 p.m., 7–11 p.m.

Experience Karnataka

SHOPPING

From heavy south Indian silk saris to hand-crafted accessories, the option of picking up some souvenirs are immense.

AMBARA
Find a curated collection of jewellery, bags, clothing, textiles and home accessories along with a plant nursery and a café, on the fringes of the Ulsoor Lake.
22, Annaswamy Mudaliar Road, Ulsoor; Ph-080 2557 5196; 10.30am–7pm

ANTS
For Bodo weaves, bamboo baskets, black pottery, footwear, jewellery and more, make way to the shelves of this Ants Craft Trust initiative. The bric-a-bracs are sourced largely from craftsmen of the northeastern states of India. The trust is focused on providing sustained livelihood and a platform to market these products. Ants also runs a café on the first floor (9.30 a.m.–8.30 p.m.).
2286, 1st Cross, 14th A Main, HAL II Stage, Indiranagar, Bengaluru; Ph: 080-41715639; www.theantstore.com; Timings: 10.30 a.m.–8 p.m.

APAULOGY CURIOUS ILLUSTRATION
Transport yourself to the laid-back life and times of Bengaluru with cartoonist Paul Fernandes' depiction of the city when riding a cycle in the dark, minus a kerosene oil lamp, was a serious crime. History enthusiasts will be immersed in this unique gallery that brings alive the old institutions of the city! Pick up original prints (₹1,300–2,500) or bookmarks to take home a slice of Bengaluru.
15, Clarke Road, Opp. Au Bon Pain, Richards Park Entrance, Richards Park, Bengaluru; Ph: 08105436700; www.paulfernandes.in; Timings: 11 a.m.–7 p.m., Sun: Noon–7 p.m. Call before going there.

ARASTAN
A unique range of exclusive hand-crafted collectibles like carpets, jewellery, lamps, wall art and more are sourced from the artisans on the ancient silk route. This is meant for discerning tourists who are not looking to stretch the buck.
Nandidurga Road, Jayamahal Extension, Bengaluru; Ph: 09900026956; Timings: 10.30 a.m.–6.30 p.m.

CAUVERY ARTS & CRAFT EMPORIUM
It is a promise that you will have to be torn away from Cauvery without buying! An easy claim to make with a vast range of prices in products like silver jewellery, inlay work, clothes, toys, bags, curios in brass and sandalwood, elaborate furniture and shawls. An option of a flexible budget and shipping facility for large goods, counter-balances non-persuasive sales staff and an overwhelming selection on display.
49, MG Road, Bengaluru; Ph: 080-25581118; www.cauverycrafts.com; Timings: 10 a.m.–8.30 p.m.

CHICKPET AND AVENUE ROAD
This 400-year-old market is a pulsating cauldron of shopping buzz. Manoeuvre past hectic shoppers into the narrow streets sprinkled with old temples.

Our picks include the famous and authentic **Balaji Antiques**, the first shop that started selling gramophones in the state and a sari pilgrimage of the oldest shops here. Get lost in the sea of weathered antiques, collected from all over India at Balaji's (1924).
64, Balaji Silk Complex, 1st Floor, Avenue Road, Opp. Bhagaram Sweets, Bengaluru; Ph: 09342410288; www.balajiantiques.com; Timings: 11 a.m.–7.30 p.m., Sundays closed.

To get lost in metres of embellished silks and cottons, step into the 90-year-old **Rukmini Hall** or **Shankari Mahalakshmi Hall**, which started in 1913 amongst many others.

- Rukmini Hall, 711-712, Chickpet, Bengaluru; Ph: 080-22254938; Timings: 11 a.m.–7.30 p.m.
- Shankari Mahalakshmi Hall, 218, Chickpet, Bengaluru; Ph: 080-41242926; Timings: 10.30 a.m.–8.30 p.m.

CHUMBAK
Bengaluru-based Chumbak has taken the country by storm with their Indian-themed, kitsch collectables. The store at CMH Road is the largest with maximum choice.
520, Chinmaya Mission Hospital Rd, Indira Nagar 1st Stage, H Colony, Indiranagar; Ph: 080 6900 1520; Timings: 10 a.m.–9 p.m.

CINNAMON
For an exclusive collection of lifestyle products, head to Cinnamon, which lies in a beautiful earthy bungalow off Ulsoor.
24, Gangadhar Chetty Road; Ph: 080 2536 7888; Timings: 10.30 a.m.–8.15 p.m.

COMMERCIAL STREET
Sharpen your bargaining skills at Bengaluru's shopping hotspot, **Commercial Street** where you can get everything under the sun. Or so it seems. Find branded clothes, jewellery, furnishings, silver, shoes, trinkets and more in narrow cramped streets, and the famous sari haven, **Mysore Sari Udyog** are some recommendations. Down a few parallel streets, **Shivaji Nagar** is yet another landmark area which houses the famous fruit and flower market, **Russel Market** (Timings: 6.30 a.m.–9 p.m.) and the 1932-built **Beef Market** (Timings: 7 a.m.–10 p.m.).
- **The Silver Shop**, 28, Commercial Street, Bengaluru; Ph: 09845128759; Timings: 10.30 a.m.–2.30 p.m., 4–8.30 p.m., Sun: Noon–2 p.m., 4–7 p.m.
- **Asiatic Arts & Crafts** (for antiques), 133/2, Commercial Street, Bengaluru; Ph: 080-41517915.

FANCY CHILLI
Photo-frames, metal signages, mugs, tissue holders and boho-art make for quirky gifts. Head to no other place other than Fancy Chilli.
552, 2nd Floor, 22nd Cross, 14th Main Rd, Sector 3, HSR Layout; Ph: 096110 33334; Timings: 10.30 a.m.–9 p.m.

LEVITATE
Boho apparel, kitschy knick-knacks, silver and costume jewellery and much more is cramped in a cosy room of the 100 ft. restaurant. Biker and an aficionado of all things handcrafted, Meghna Khanna steers the business and Bengaluru's taste into stunning jewellery, bright-coloured shoes and unique accessories and more to design your own style.
Mezzanine Floor, 100 ft. Boutique Restaurant, 777/I, 100 Feet Road, Indiranagar, Bengaluru; Ph: 080-64528190; Timings: 11 a.m.–9.30 p.m.

THE ORANGE BICYCLE
The lifestyle store offers fun gifting ideas – think cushions, clothes, planters, clocks, wall hangings, accessories and more – and is definitely one of the most popular picks for Bangloreans.
5th Cross Road, Doopanahalli; Ph; 080 50399365; Timings: 11 a.m.–7.30 p.m. (Mondays closed)

TURTLE DOVES
Your one-stop shop for kitsch collectibles, Turtle Doves adds a little twist to shopping.
198/C, 7th Main Road, 3rd Block Jayanagar, Near NMKRV College; Ph: 097416 26739; Timings: 10 a.m.–8 p.m.

Experience Karnataka

DAY TRIPS *from* BENGALURU

*B*engaluru is one of the few metros, from where a number of day trips fill up the weekends for travel enthusiasts. Nandi Hills, Lepakshi Temple, Hessarghatta and some atmospheric resorts make a great destination to unwind – even if it's only to recharge and get back to work. Here are the top ten suggestions to drive out and explore places around the city.

Road travel has gained popularity over the years

NANDI HILLS

60km | 2hrs. (Approx.)

Get onto NH7, Bengaluru–Hyderabad Highway beyond the Kempegowda International Airport. Cross Devanahalli and take the prominent left to Nandi Hills. From the Karahalli Cross T-point, take left for the hills and right for Nandi town and Bhoganandeeshwara Temple.

Only 60km from Bengaluru, Nandi Hills is an ancient hill fortress, which was built during the Chola period. It goes by several names, the most common ones being Ananda Giri meaning 'The Hill of Happiness' and Nandi Hills owing to the Nandidurga Fort built here by the ruler Tipu Sultan. Representing the most popular day trip off the city, the hill rises towards the sky from flat surroundings, distinguishing itself immediately. Nandi Hills is flanked by Channa Giri and Brahmagiri Hills, together offering a vast craggy expanse to climb and watch the clouds below you. The 2,000-feet-high rock hill makes a great early morning drive, with the crisp cold air engulfing you.

Bangaloreans should be ever grateful to Tipu Sultan, who fortified this hill and used it as his summer home, giving it a lease of life that one would have never imagined. Even the Britishers followed suit and used this as a haven to enjoy the salubrious climate here. Now, a number of tourists and regulars drop in to see the sightseeing points like Tipu's Drop, Yoganandeeshwara Temple, Amrita Sarovar, Nehru Nilaya and the Bhoganandeeshwara Temple on the foothills. A small café is famous for dishing out plates of Maggi and steaming cups of *chai* for the visitors.

◀ View from Nandi Hills

LEPAKSHI

120km | 3-4hrs. (Approx.)

Follow NH7 from the city right up to Bagepalli, from where the road swerves left straight to Lepakshi. If you are on the Kodur Road, you are on the right track.

Though situated just across the border of Karnataka in Anantpur district of Andhra Pradesh, Lepakshi Temple makes for a brilliant heritage trip for history enthusiasts. A 120-km drive from Bengaluru lands you in the midst of exquisite shrines dedicated to Shiva, Vishnu and Veerabhadra, which were built during the Vijayanagar period (1336–1646). Apart from these shrines, the Lepakshi Nandi gets hundreds of eyeballs each day. It is a granite monolithic sculpture, located 200 metres from the main temple. It is 4.5 metres high and 8.23 metres long – a staggering size for a statue – making it one of the largest Nandis in India. A trip to Lepakshi eludes any religious motives. It is best explored for its intricate designs and the famous craftsmanship portrayed in the Vijayanagar-style of architecture. It is a worthy testament to the imagination and sculpting prowess of the Vijayanagar period. The carvings on each pillar and the unique murals that adorn the temple complex are truly stunning. The main Veerabhadraswamy Temple was built in 1538 by Virupanna, the treasurer of the empire. It encloses five different shrines, dedicated to different gods, including Naga and Durga. It is said that the temple practically emptied the wealth of the empire with its over-the-top grandeur. As a punishment, the king decided to stop construction and ordered Virupanna to be blinded. Hearing this, the treasurer himself ripped his eyes and threw them at the temple, leaving two stains on the walls of the *kalyana mandapa* (marriage hall). Legend goes that it is because of this that the town was christened Lepakshi – or the 'village of blinded eyes'.

BHEEMESHWARI

100km | 2-3hrs. (Approx.)

Take the Kanakpura–Kollegal Highway from Bengaluru. Turn at Halagur to take the Halagur–Muttatti Road, until you reach Bheemeshwari Camp.

Trekking, coracle ride, birdwatching, ziplining, mountain biking, rope walking, rafting and kayaking are some of the activities to look forward to, when visiting the Bheemeshwari Camp off Bengaluru. One of the easiest outdoor getaways for locals, this promises a day of adventure and tryst with nature. The Bheemeshwari Camp is run by Jungle Lodges & Resorts, which aims to offer a wholesome outdoor experience to guests. One can stay overnight in tents, but a day is ample to explore along River Cauvery. Close enough from the city, and yet delightfully aloof, the destination is a good, quick way to reinvigorate from city life. The best time to go there is just after monsoons, as the terrain breaks into a million shades of green and offers a decidedly refreshing experience.

HESSARGHATTA

35km | 1.5hrs. (Approx.)

Take NH4 (Tumkur Road) and look out for the Reliance building on your right after hitting the Peenya industrial area. Take the right at this building, and follow the signs for the next 8km. A hand-drawn map on the site of Nrityagram can be downloaded and comes in handy.

Hessarghatta offers twin experiences of exploring the gorgeous campus of Nrityagram Dance School started by Odissi exponent, Protima Bedi, and a lunch at Taj Kuteeram. An excellent educational and relaxing alternative to a packed weekend, this one-day trip helps to experience a unique *gurukul* system for dance, in a scenic backdrop. The nature-inspired architecture by Gerard De Cunha for both properties blends seamlessly in the rural setting.

Built by late Protima Bedi, who set out to revive the *gurukul* system of dance education for seven classical forms, Nrityagram was started in 1990. Shaped from simple material and natural surroundings, the structure exudes a calming ambience to learn an art form. Even after Protima Bedi's tragic death, the school continues to follow her dream, where dancers can reach perfection. It is now led by Lynne Fernandez and only holds Odissi classes.

A temple dedicated to Protima Bedi's teacher, Guru Kelucharan Mohapatra stands on one side of the yoga platform as one enters the school. You can walk around and explore the property after taking a quick permission from the reception; it is advisable to call and let them know first. Organic vegetable gardens, rock benches and the shade of trees keep you company.

The highlight of the trip is the opportunity to see young dance students take to the stage during their classes. Guests are allowed on specific days to watch the practise sessions led by Surupa Sen and Bijayani Satpathy. International and Indian students, dressed in typical bordered cotton saris and *bindis* – men in traditional *dhotis* – move rhythmically for over two hours.

Entry Fee: Adults/Children/Foreigners: ₹*50;* ***Timings****: 10 a.m.–2 p.m., Tuesday to Saturday (Dance classes are only between 10.30 a.m. & 1 p.m.)*

Kuteeram, the accommodation of Nrityagram, was taken over by the Taj Group. The adjacent property is

Experience Karnataka

also the creation of Gerard De Cunha, and follows the same design language. If you are not staying a night, do book a lunch at the in-house restaurant.

SHIVANASAMUDRA WATERFALLS

139km | 3hrs. (Approx.)

Drive along NH209 and take a left from Malavalli.

A post-monsoon must, head 139km southwest towards Malavalli from where the road leads to the frothy Shivanasamudra Waterfalls. Originating from the Cauvery River, small streams make their way from across the Deccan Plateau to converge here and plummet down a height of almost 100 metres. The wide falls have coverage of 305 metres across, making it a mammoth waterfall. The twin segment on the left make for the Gaganachukki Falls and the section on the right is known as the Bharachukki Falls. The best time to visit the falls is from July to October, when the white wall of water makes for a spectacular sight. It is best not to get too close to the falls as unpredictable water movements often result in deaths, but the most vantage spot for photo opportunities lies in the

▼ Thousands of tourists flock to see the splendid Gaganachukki Falls

Shivanasamudra watchtower. The trip makes for a great drive along the Karnataka countryside and watching the magical waterfalls at your destination.

GALIBORE

 100km | 2-3hrs. (Approx.)

Get on the Kanakapura Road from the city and take a left from Kanakapura Junction towards Sangam. At Sangam, look out for a rusty Galibore board. From here, it's 9km on an off-tar experience until you reach the camp.

An easy drive of 100km from the city, Galibore is pleasantly camouflaged between the Cauvery River and the thick forest of the Cauvery Wildlife Sanctuary. Taken over by the Jungle Lodges & Resorts, the campsite sits at the edge of the river and was earlier known for angling. Since angling (even the catch and release system) has been banned, tourists come here to get their adventure fix with guided activities like rafting, trekking and kayaking. An ideal backdrop for an outdoor experience of living in tents and community camp activities, this can be extended to an overnight stay. Galibore is a great place to connect with nature and unplug from city life. You will have to disconnect your

Experience Karnataka

phone (there is no signal), Internet and TV to immerse in solitude. Kayaking, hiking, rafting, mountain biking and birdwatching are on the cards at Galibore. There are 12 thatched-roofed, tented cottages, furnished amply with a double bed, clothes rack, table fan and a dresser. The olive-green tents are made to blend with the jungle. The bathrooms are attached to the tent but with a separate entrance. Fixed menus of veg and non-veg meals are served in the common gazebo at designated timings.

TOP TIP: It's difficult to find guides here, so you can contact Mr Ramakrishna, an approved guide (Ph: 09945645237), to understand the legends associated with the temple.

SOMANATHAPURA

150km | 1.5hrs. (Approx.)

Leave for Mysore Road from the city and stay on it till Maddur. Take a left at Maddur on SH17 and reach Malavalli. The distance on direction boards is frustratingly wrong and it is best to take directions/seek help from local villagers.

A trip to discover the wonder of Hoysala temples is incomplete without a trip to Somanathapura – this is the third-most important structure after the Halebeedu and Belur temples. The thirteenth-century temple is an exquisite representation of the characteristic Hoysala architecture. People often give this a miss, as it is a directional deviation from the popular Belur–Halebeedu sector, but the Keshava Temple (Vishnu) built in AD 1268 at Somanathapura should not be given a miss. Comparable in grandeur and architecture, this one, in fact, is closer to Bengaluru and hardly treaded. The typical soapstone structure is one of the 92 temples in Karnataka, which were built under

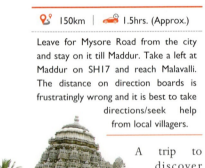

The magnificent Hoysala temples at Somanathapura ▲

the Hoysala regime. Five hundred artisans created the 5,000 intricate statues over a period of 58 years. You will find a number of themes ranging from Mahabharata, Ramayana, folk-tales and eroticism; a good way to educate people in the absence of schools. The things to take special notice of include the pillars of the temple, platform on which it stands, the three statues dedicated to Vishnu, 16 different ceilings and Janardhan's belly.

CHITRADURGA

203km | 4-5hrs. (Approx.)

Catch NH4 from Bengaluru. Turn left onto the Medhehalli Road, a kilometre before Chitradurga town.

The Chitradurga Fort dates back to the time of the Mahabharata, when the demon brother–sister duo, Hidimba and Hidimbi, lived on this hill. According to legend, in an altercation with the Pandavas, Bhima killed the brother. Bhima then married the demon sister and had a son with her, Ghatotkacha, who played a vital role in the Mahabharata war. Eons later, the fort was presented to Timmana Nayaka, a military serviceman of the Vijayanagar Empire in the sixteenth century. The Nayaka family occupied the fort for over a century, before it fell in the hands of Hyder Ali. The bouldery terrain of the region is dramatic, especially if one is standing atop the fort hill. Apart from the fort, one can visit the ancient Chandravalli Caves. A day trip is sufficient to visit both the fort and the caves.

Hiring a guide is recommended as then you will get to hear anecdotes and learn the interesting elements of this historical site. At the fort, an elephant memorial, a Ganesha temple, oil tanks, an ancient gym, a humongous 32-feet swing and elaborate *mantapas* (pandals) are the highlights. You can also climb to the highest tower of the fort, but only if you are agile and physically fit for unsupported rock climbing. There are practically no steps. A local climbing wonder, Jyothi Raj (pg. 177), is often seen showing off his climbing prowess near the first few gates. He is famous for climbing without any gear or accessories. If you are lucky, you will see him in action. (**Entry Fee**: Indians: ₹5, Foreigner: ₹100; **Timings**: 6 a.m.–6 p.m.)

Two other places can also be visited on the same trip.

Situated at a distance of 4km from Chitradurga, the Chandravalli Caves look unimpressive from the outside, but hoard a vast amount of history in the statues, Shivlinga and many other daily use objects that were found here during excavation. There is an 80-feet drop, which you can walk down to. An Ankali Mutt Temple stands below a huge rock just outside the caves. Situated 32km

Experience Karnataka

before Chitradurga, the Van Vilas Sagar Dam (also known as Mari Kanive) stands at the end of a fantastic drive through windmill-flanked low hills. The dam is a picturesque spot and worth the detour. A drive through the rustic countryside leads to the top of the dam from where you can get a clear view of the rushing water below.

RANGANATHITTU BIRD SANCTUARY

135km | 3hrs. (Approx.)

This lies on NH275 after you cross Ramnagar, Channpatna and Mandya.

Birding enthusiasts will be easily lured into a day trip to the Ranganathittu Bird Sanctuary on way to Mysuru. In fact, this – it lies in the Mandya district, just 3km before Srirangapatnam – is the largest bird sanctuary in the state. It spreads over a meagre 0.67km^2 in area, and comprises six islets on the banks of the Cauvery River. But this is big enough to draw the attention of a number of species of birds. In fact, the islets were formed only when an embankment was built across the Cauvery River in 1648, by the then Mysore king, Kanteerava Narasimharaja Wodeyar. The ideal time to visit the sanctuary is in the winter months, from December to February, when as many as over 40,000 birds (including migratory ones) congregate here. It is a popular nesting site for them. One is likely to spot the painted stork, Asian openbill stork, common spoonbill, woolly-necked stork,

Ranganathittu Bird Sanctuary hosts a large number of exotic migratory species

black-headed ibis, lesser whistling duck, Indian shag, stork-billed kingfisher, egret, cormorant, Oriental darter, herons, the great stone plover and river tern here. Start your trip with a 45-minute documentary by Dr Salim Ali and then head out on a boat or along the water body on foot.

TALAKKAD

136km | 3hrs. (Approx.)

Take NH948 and take left from Malavalli Road to Talakkad.

A spectacular insipid terrain sprawls on the edge of Cauvery River, about 133km away from Bengaluru. The once cluster of thirty temples, now lies partially below the sandy banks. Legend goes that twin brothers, Tala and Kadu, once saw wild elephants worshipping a tree, which contained an image of Shiva. The brothers started cutting the tree, only to discover that the elephants were sages. As soon as they cut the tree, it was miraculously restored. There are two stone images in front of the Veerabhadraswamy Temple, which are said to represent the brothers. Much later, this was also one of the pit stops for Lord Rama on his way to Lanka.

Another legend of the seventeenth century surrounds the temples. In 1610, the Mysore king conquered the town, when the previous king was visiting the temples to pray for relief from an incurable disease. He left Srirangapatnam in charge of his wife, Rani Alamelamma. Hearing that her husband was on the verge of passing away – on account of his illness – she left for Talakkad to see him once before his death, handing over Srirangapatnam to the Wodeyar king of Mysore. The Wodeyar king sent an army after the rani to seize her jewels. To protect herself, Rani Alamelamma jumped into the Kaveri River (that skirts the temple), cursing the Wodeyar king: 'Let Talakkad become sand; let Malangi become a whirlpool; let the Mysore Rajas fail to beget heirs.' Talakkad did get submerged in the sand and the Wodeyar dynasty has dwindled over the years on account of not having a proper heir.

Visit here to see the excellent architecture and transport yourself to centuries ago, for a complete historic immersion.

Mysuru

A view of Mysuru city, the city of magnificent temples, palaces and gardens

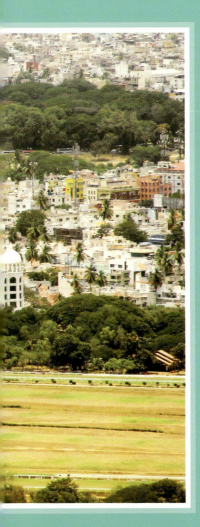

VITALS
Getting There
Mysuru lies 146km (approx. 3 hours) from Bengaluru, at the end of the arterial SH17, which further wends towards Kabini, Kodagu and the Nilgiris. The highway is smooth with plenty of pit stops to take a break and detour. The city is also well connected by train and multiple options of buses.

Mysuru can be pegged as the cultural capital of the state, given its vibrant history. Located in the shadow of the Chamundi Hill, this is the second-largest city of Karnataka, and the erstwhile capital of the state. Considered a handicraft destination of Karnataka, Mysuru is world renowned for its silk, gold foil work on paintings, sandalwood, inlay work and, now, yoga. A trip to the city is imperative as an orientation to Karnataka. You are likely to hit it time and again, on several trips off Bengaluru as the SH17 connects other drive-friendly destinations around.

Best Time to Go
The cooler months from October to February are ideal for sightseeing, though a trip planned around the Mysore Dusshera will add an exciting flavour to your trip.

Experience Karnataka

EXPLORING THE CITY

The characteristic heritage ambience of Mysuru can be attributed to the long-ruling Wodeyar family (16th century onwards) of the region. They were great patrons of music, crafts and art forms. The mould that Mysuru was fit in, still lives on till date. The city still resonates this passion for arts, in its many museums and cultural events. However, the contribution of Hyder Ali and son, Tipu Sultan (18th century) cannot be diminished for the city. It was then that the city reached the pinnacle of its military power, withstanding constant conflicts with the Marathas, British and the Nizams from south of India.

Political and military events took a full circle when Tipu Sultan died in the Fourth Anglo-Mysore War in 1799, and the British re-instated the Wodeyar rulers, and became a princely state under the British India Empire.

Reserve ample days to explore the palace, the main highlight of the city, Chamundeshwari Temple, art galleries, Brindavan Gardens and a peek into the Mysuru silk factories.

SIGHTSEEING HIGHLIGHTS
Mysore Palace

The exquisite architecture of late nineteenth-century Indo-Saracenic aesthetics can be seen in the Mysore Palace, the single-most jaw-droppingly beautiful structure in the

▼ Mysore Palace: The official residence of the Wodeyar rajas

SNAP THE RIGHT MOMENTS
ACROSS KARNATAKA

Thread the romantic paths of the state and rediscover its treasures when you stay at our premium heritage resorts & hotels offering a unique journey of modern conveniences, centric locations within the comfort of luxury.

Now Present in
Mysore • Hampi • Shimoga • Dandeli

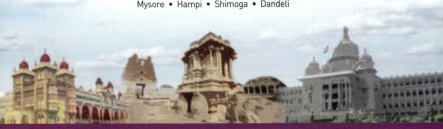

Reservations Call: +91 80 41276667 / 9845176667

Across India: Amritsar • Ahmedabad • Bangalore • Bharuch • Bhuj • Chandigarh • Dehradun • Goa
Gurgaon • Haridwar • Jaipur • Kolkata • Mussoorie • Mahabaleshwar • Navi Mumbai • Pune
Rajkot • Santiniketan • Udaipur • Vadodara • Nairobi

SAFE ROADS MAKE A HAPPY CITY

RULES OF THE ROAD

USE A SEATBELT | OBEY TRAFFIC SIGNALS | DON'T DRINK AND DRIVE | WEAR A HELMET | FOLLOW LANE DISCIPLINE

Initiated By

FOLLOW THE RTR TROUPE
 @respecttheroad

JOIN THE CONVERSATION
 Facebook.com/respecttheroad

city. Keep aside at least a few hours to roam the large gardens, grey granite rooms and the museum-esque rooms inside. All this after going through the towering tiered entrances. Be prepared to stand in queue as thousands visit the palace each day. Known as Amba Vilas, this is the official residence of the erstwhile royals of Mysuru. Apart from the royal paraphernalia, the palace has 12 Hindu temples. The Shwetha Varahaswamy Temple, Prasanna Krishnaswamy Temple, Lakshmiramana Swamy Temple and the Trineshwara Swamy Temple are worth a visit. Arrive in the evening to see the temples beautifully lit up. If you are travelling with kids, the elephant and camel rides (₹40) may provide a break in the history-filled day.

Sunday nights and public holidays are especially worth your while as the palace is lit up with thousands of bulbs.

Entry Fee*: Adults: ₹40, Children (10–18yrs): ₹20, Children (below 10yrs): ₹10;* ***Camera****: Free;* ***Timings****: 10 a.m.–5.30 p.m.*

St Philomena's Church is one of the most popular churches of Karnataka

St Philomena's Church

This Gothic-styled structure stands in contrast to the nuances of the Mysore Palace but is a building that one should not miss. The stained glass windows of AD 1840 and 175-feet twin towers makes St Philomena's Church one of the most striking churches of Karnataka. The church houses a cellar where a statue of St Philomena as a holy saint

Experience Karnataka

reclines. She is depicted similarly as in the third century in Greece. A piece of her bone and clothes are also kept safely here.

Timings: 8 a.m.–6 p.m.

Brindavan Gardens & KRS Dam

The KRS or Krishna Raja Sagara Dam is almost a century old but still holds sway to one of the most traversed areas of the city. After all, the dam and the surrounding gardens make for the lungs of Mysuru, giving locals and visitors an opportunity to step away from the city bustle and relax. The Brindavan Gardens are located 12km northwest of Mysuru and are known for a sprawling expanse of green with rows of colourful fountains. Boating, advanced lighting techniques with the movement of water in the fountains and the dam areas are the highlights. Rivers Kaveri, Hemavathi and Lakshmana Tirtha converge here. The site has been forever immortalized by Kannada movies.

Timings: 10 a.m.–8 p.m.

Chamundeshwari Temple

This hilltop temple is dedicated to the family goddess of the Mysuru royals, Chamundeshwari. But first you have to meet the gaudy, bright,

▼ The Chamundi *gopuram* stands tall in the distance

The statue of Mahishasura towers over its surroundings

statue of Mahishasura, so you can understand what Chamundeshwari Devi was up against, when she began to fight with him. He holds a sword, a serpent and wears a menacing expression on his face. Further ahead on the left, the yellow carved *gopuram* (an ornate, monumental tower at the entrance of a temple) with seven tiers becomes progressively magnificent as you approach it. The Dravidian-style temple complex surrounds a small shrine, which you can enter through a large, silver gate. The quadrangular structure houses the main silver doorway, entrance, Navaranga Hall, Antharala Mantapa, sanctum sanctorum and Prakara. A small flagstaff and a stone with imprints of the goddess' feet is your first sight inside. A small Nandi statue faces the shrine. One has to loop around to the left and get ushered onto a wooden platform to see the deity. There is also a 6-feet statue of Maharaja Krishnaraja Wodeyar III along with many other framed paintings of the Durga.

Timings: *7.30 a.m–9 p.m.*

Jagmohan Palace

This erstwhile royal auditorium was built in 1861. Lying just west of the Mysore Palace, the Jagmohan Palace houses the Jayachamarajendra Art Gallery. Three floors of massive

Experience Karnataka

collections of Indian paintings, including works by noted artist Raja Ravi Varma and traditional Japanese art, this will interest the museum and art enthusiasts. Weapons and rare musical instruments also occupy some of the display units.

Timings: 8.30 a.m.–5 p.m.

Government Silk Factory

The Government Silk Factory in Mysuru is the only place in the city where you can see the entire process of silk spinning, soaking, weaving and finally dyeing to create special designs. Opt for a guided tour to transport yourself into a world of *zaris* (embroidery work), colours and reams of fabric. A chance to interact with the master weavers is ensured. You can also shop here after the tour.

Timings: 7.30 a.m.–4 p.m.

Mysore Zoo

The Mysore Zoo, or officially the Sri Chamarajendra Zoological Gardens, is a 157-acre expanse in the middle of the city. An imperative addition to the itinerary if you are travelling with children, there are a number of enclosures and even a

Leopard cubs play as they are watched over by their mother in the Mysore Zoo

lake inside the premises. Expect to see anacondas, giraffes, zebras, lions, tigers, white rhinoceroses and baboons, along with many other avian species.

*Entry Fee: Adults: ₹50, Children: (above 4yrs.):₹20; **Camera**:₹150; **Battery Vehicle**:₹150; **Timings**: 8.30 a.m.–5.30 p.m., Tuesdays closed.*

Devaraja Market

A flower and vegetable special, this one is top on the list of photography enthusiasts. The market lies along the Sayyaji Rao Road and has two entrances – the north entrance faces the Dufferin Clock Tower and the south entrance is on the Dhanvantri Road. Visit here to be consumed by the city bustle.

ACCOMMODATION

THE GREEN HOTEL
Old-world charm comes alive at the Green Hotel's heritage vibe, al fresco seating and spacious rooms.
2270, Vinoba Road, Jayalakshmipuram, Mysuru;
Ph: 0821-4255000;
Tariff: ₹3,500 onwards.

HOTEL REGAALIS
The 4 acres of lush landscape gives a relief when you enter from the crowded streets of Mysuru. Well-appointed rooms and excellent service make Hotel Regaalis a good choice.
13-14, Vinoba Road, Mysuru; Ph: 0821-2426426;
www.ushalexushotels.com;
Tariff: ₹3,500–5,500 plus taxes.

JASMINE APARTMENT SUITES
Jasmine is a good pick if you do not want to stay close to the touristy clutter. The suites are comfortable and clean, equipped with a kitchenette – perfect for an independence-loving tourist.
83, 2nd B Cross 2nd Main, Vijayanagar, Mysuru;
Ph: 09986032976; www.mcijasminesuites.com;
Tariff: ₹2,000 plus taxes.

LALITHA MAHAL PALACE HOTEL
Choose Lalitha Mahal for a stunning location near the Chamundi Temple. More so, the maharaja built this in 1927 for the use of the viceroy. The ornate elements still live on in the building.
Lalitha Mahal Quatras, Mysuru;
Ph: 0821-2470444; www.lalithamahalpalace.in;
Tariff: ₹4,000 onwards.

ROYAL ORCHID METROPOLE
Another stalwart on the hospitality scape, Royal Orchid is fashioned from a colonial era building with lavish rooms and al fresco dining. A swimming pool is an additional plus.
5, Jhansi Lakshmibai Road, Mysuru;
Ph: 0821-4255566; www.royalorchidhotels.com;
Tariff: ₹3,600 plus taxes.

WINDFLOWER SPA AND RESORTS
The lure of plush rooms, spa and the credibility of the brand is what brings the tourists to Windflower. It is conveniently located close to the sightseeing areas of the city.
295, Maharanapratap Road, Nazarbad, Mysuru;
Ph: 080-41142408; www.thewindflower.com;
Tariff: ₹5,850–16,200 plus taxes.

EATING OUT

DOWN TOWN
Fast-food cravings will be put to rest at Down Town with a choice of non-veg burgers, rolls and hot dogs – with a tinge of home-cooked styled elements.
42, Chandra Complex, VV Mohalla, Kalidasa Road, Jayalakshmipuram, Mysuru; Ph: 0821-2513942; Timings: 11.45 a.m.–2.30 p.m., 5.30–10 p.m.; Meal for 2: Below ₹250.

GREEN LEAF FOOD COURT
Speedy service, south Indian meals, and a perfect location to satiate hunger pangs are assured at Green Leaf.
12th Cross, Kalidasa Road, Near ICICI Bank, Vani Vilas Mohalla, Mysuru; Ph: 0821-6550857; Timings: 7.30 a.m.–10.30 p.m.; Meal for 2: ₹250–500.

LE GARDENIA
Regaalis' multi-cuisine restaurant offers a large selection of dishes. This is one of the swishiest joints in town.
13-14, Vinoba Road, Mysuru; Ph: 0821-2426426; Timings: 11 a.m.–11 p.m.; Meal for 2: ₹500–750.

MALGUDI CAFÉ
Located in the Green Hotel, Malgudi Café is best known for its filter coffee and cakes made by a self-help group.
2270, Vinoba Road, Jayalakshmipuram, Mysuru; Ph: 0821-4255000; Timings: 10 a.m.–7 p.m.; Meal for 2: ₹250–500.

MUST DO MUST SEE
Royal Mysore Walks

With an aim to present an authentic image of the city, Royal Mysore Walks organizes customized and pre-scheduled walks for visitors, according to the themes that they are interested in. The well-researched and impeccably delivered information draws you into the cultural capital in no time – food, history and living culture are the highlights. Opt for offbeat tours to really understand Mysuru. Apart from walking tours, you can also opt for jeep or cycling trips. (www.royalmysorewalks.com; customized pricing depending on the group size.)

Mysore Dusshera

One of the most celebrated occasions of the state, the Mysore Dusshera changes the calm rhythm of the city into a pulsating one. Of the ten days that precede the Dusshera are the Navaratri, of which the sixth day is most important. On this day, Goddess Saraswathi is worshipped in a special puja. Similarly, the eighth day is dedicated to Goddess Durga and the ninth day to Goddess Lakshmi. On these days, you will find activities centred on the city temples that are dedicated to goddesses. On the first day of the celebrations, the royal couple flags off the period with a small ceremony at the hilltop Chamundeshwari Temple. All throughout the ten days,

Mysore Dusshera: A tusker carrying the golden palanquin of Goddess Chamundeshwari

one of the key highlights is the illuminating of the palace with close to 1,00,000 lamps. Various artistes perform in the religious and cultural programmes that are held in front of the illuminated palace. Dances and musical performances enthral the audience. Two hours (7–9 p.m.) have been designated for the first eight days and then three hours (7–10 p.m.) for the final Vijayadashami day. Different cultural programmes and exhibitions keep the city abuzz; the Dusshera Exhibition, which is held opposite the Mysore Palace, was initiated by Chamaraja Wodeyar X in 1880. People, both residents of the city and tourists, throng the different stalls in this exhibition that sells

An artiste dressed as Lord Hanuman, during Mysore Dusshera

eatables, cosmetics, clothes, and kitchenware among others. However, it is the grand finale that is the most exquisite of sights. The Jamboo Savari (elephant parade) is what everyone waits for. This starts from the Mysore Palace with the idol of Goddess Chamundeshwari – on a golden *mantapa* – being carried on a caparisoned elephant, all the way up to Bannimantap. Music and dance troupes, music bands, horses and camels, beautiful tableaux are a part of the procession as the elephants amble down the main road, flanked by visitors. To end the celebrations, a torch light parade is held on the Bannimantap grounds, and the banni tree is worshiped. In the days of yore, kings would worship the banni tree before going to war, in order to return victorious. Fireworks go on late into the night.

DETOUR
Cheluvanarayana Swamy Temple, Melkote

The hilltop Vaishnavite village of Melkote (53km from Mysuru) is an ancient region, with the Cheluvanarayana Swamy Temple as the central attraction. Also known as Yadugiri, the rock scape is home to the temple of Yoganarasimha Swamy. Since saint Sri Ramanujacharya stayed in this village in the twelfth century, everything here is themed after him. A black, serene statue of Lord Vishnu draped in saffron stands inside the dark complex of Cheluvanarayana Swamy Temple. Outside the main sanctum, the intricately carved pillars and other shrines dedicated to his avatars (reincarnations) hold the attention of tourists. The outer walls of the temples have carvings of the *dasavavatars* (ten incarnations) on them.

Timings: 8.30 a.m.–1 p.m., 4–6 p.m., 7–8.30 p.m.

A Narsimhaswamy shrine lies on top of a hill overlooking the village. You can get here by road, but you have to cover the last stretch on foot. From here, you can get a bird's eye view of the whole village. It is said that Lord Rama, Lord Krishna and Lord Brahma meditated here at different times. Inside, the deity has a peaceful expression as compared to the ferocious form of Narsimhaswamy.

Timings: 9.30 a.m.–1.30 p.m., 5–7.30 p.m.

Incidentally, Melkote is also the birthplace of Jayalalitha, the chief minister of Tamil Nadu.

Sri Ranganathaswamy Temple, Srirangapatnam

A Vaishnavite shrine, close to the city of Mysuru (22km), the Sri Ranganathaswamy lies in Srirangapatnam. You can visit this temple on the same trip as Melkote. Inside the high stonewalls lie a black stone statue of a sleeping Lord Vishnu. The complex is relatively big and houses other shrines dedicated to Vishnu, along with Garuda, Krishna and Tirupati. On your way out, you can buy *prasadam* (offerings to the deity), a combination of dry fruits, orange *shakkar* (sugar) and laddoos.

Timings: *7.30 a.m.–1.30 p.m., 4–8 p.m.*

Srikanteshwara Swamy Temple, Nanjangud

A short detour of 23km from Mysuru will take you to the holy abode of Srikanteshwara Swamy or the Nanjundeshwara (Lord Shiva) Temple, built by the Ganga dynasty. This ninth-century temple and the town are named after Nanjundeshwara, when the lord consumed poison, as the *devas* (gods) and *asuras* (demons) churned the oceans in quest of an immortality nectar. Legend says that the product that emerged from this fervent churning was poison, which Lord Shiva consumed. The turmeric-coloured *gopuram* (an ornate, monumental tower at the entrance of a temple) rises high into the sky and a massive wooden door leads devotees inside, in a pillared complex that encloses a shrine. Inside, a granite Shivlinga is adorned with flowers. The temple lies on the opposite side of the Kappila River, which is also known as the 'Kashi of the South'.

Timings: *6 a.m.–1 p.m., 4–8.30 p.m.*

Devotees at Sri Srikanteshwara Swamy Temple

The Hoysala Trail

Picturesque setting of a Hoysala Village

Bengaluru ▸▸ Hassan ▸▸ Belur ▸▸ Halebeedu

VITALS
Getting There
Hassan lies 185km from Bengaluru on NH48. Thanks to the excellent road condition of this highway, it will not take you more than 3 hours to get to the base for tracing the Hoysala history in nearby Belur (approx. 40km from Hassan) and Halebeedu (approx. 32km from Hassan). A veritable detour on this route is the Jain pilgrimage, Shravanabelagola, which falls on the way and makes for a stop for a couple of hours. Another destination that you can add in the sector is the coffee-scaped Sakleshpur. About 40km from Hassan, this can be a stop if you have a long weekend at hand.

Best Time to Go
The cooler months from October to February are ideal to enjoy the beauty of the hot-floored Hoysala temples and climbing the hill at Shravanabelagola. Ugaadi is celebrated with much fervour. For a glimpse of local celebrations, this is a good time to plan a trip.

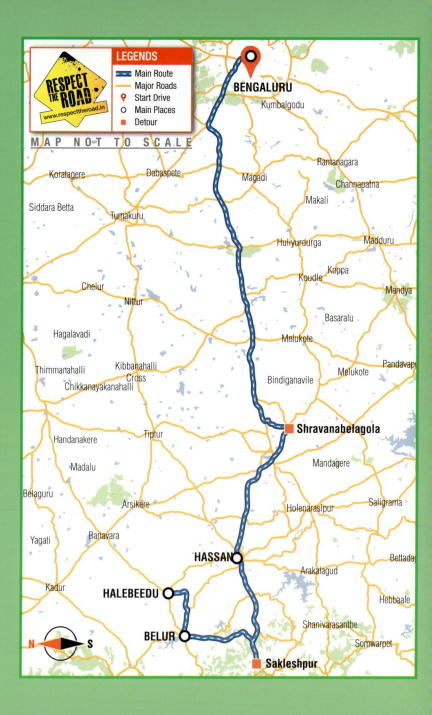

EXPLORING THE CIRCUIT

Go there to visit the two famous temples of Belur and Halebeedu, constructed during the 11th–13th-century Hoysala regime. From the 92 temples that were constructed during the period, only three were carved intricately and remain till date. These are Somanathapura (access from Mysuru), Belur and Halebeedu. Apart from the big two temples, some of the other important sites are Pushpagiri and Doddagadhavalli. The Chalukyan-influenced architecture is one of the most stunning in India and the temples reflect devotion to both Lord Shiva and Lord Vishnu. Highlights of the temple include intricate carvings and a glimpse of life between the eleventh and twelfth centuries. There is ample to see and do on this trip, especially if you are combining the Jain site of Shravanabelagola and also tracing close to 13 Hoysala sites that lie around Hassan. Hassan makes a good base to travel out, with better infrastructure in terms of stay and food. Many tourists combine the coffee town of Sakleshpur with this sector for proximity and to break the journey with a refreshing scape. Expect to be enthralled by exquisite architecture and history coming alive at these temples. The towns itself are quite small and package tourism inclined, but the countryside around them is worth your while.

SIGHTSEEING HIGHLIGHTS
Hoysaleshwara Temple, Halebeedu

At the end of the lush, manicured lawns stands this richly carved Halebeedu temple. Hire a guide to take you through this Shiva temple, which unfolds a number of stories from the epics. Surrounded by numerous ponds and lakes that add a relief to the landscape, it is similar in aesthetics to the one at Belur. The

▲ The Hoysaleshwara Temple is dedicated to Lord Shiva

Experience Karnataka

Ornate carvings in the Hoysaleshwara Temple

mythological 'seven in one animal', Makara, and tales from Ramayana and Mahabharata and Garuda pillars are the highlights. Reserve more than an hour to go through the different aspects of the temple.

Timings: Sunrise to Sunset.

Shettihalli Church

The remains of the Shettihalli Church lie 18km from Hassan and looks quite ethereal. Crumbling walls stand in the backdrop of the Gorur Dam catchment area, with the water rising to the foot of the church during monsoons – sometimes submerging it for a few feet. It is said to have been submerged in the backwaters of the Egachi–Hemavathi Dam at one point of time, but now one can walk to it. Unfortunately, not much history is available on the structure, but a trip is worth your while for photo opportunities.

Timings: Sunrise to Sunset.

Remnants of the Shettihalli Church

The facade and carvings of the Chennakesava Temple (above and below)

Chennakesava Temple, Belur

Hiring a guide at the Belur temple is a good idea as you can travel back in time with the anecdotes and legends. The star-shaped foundation of the temple is characteristic of Hoysala architecture. The temple is dedicated to Lord Vishnu and is known as the Chennakesava Temple. It took 103 years to complete its elaborate 4,000 carvings in slate stone. Replete with Hoysala emblems, statues of dancing ladies and stories of epics, the temple is sure to make you time travel. A monolithic 50-feet lamp tower greets you at the courtyard before the sanctum; it stands without support or a foundation. Threads and mirrors are used by the government-approved guides to show you the minute details of the temple. Carvings as intricate as teeth of a monkey, rotating bangles and see-through printed cloth are pointed out.

Timings: 7.30 a.m.–1 p.m., 3–7.30 p.m.

Mosale

Mosale village lies about 12km from Hassan and houses two temples dedicated to Nageshwara and Chennakesava. Many tourists give this a miss, but the simple village is a draw for those who want to step away from the crowds. These too belong to the Hoysala period but are less intricate than the main Belur and Halebeedu temples.

Timings: Sunrise to Sunset.

Gorur Dam

About 9km from Hassan stands the Gorur Dam. The dam gates are opened after the monsoons, when the white frothy water gushes out with full force. A trip here ensures a refreshing spray on the face, if you stand along the railing at the edge of the water.

Timings: 10 a.m.–5 p.m.

River Hemavathy, an important tributary of River Kaveri

The Hoysala temple at Mosale

ACCOMMODATION

THE ASHHOK HASSAN, HASSAN
This is one of the best options if you are looking for a non-resort stay in Hassan. A 24-hours' café, a bar and multiple plush-room types are highlights of the Ashhok Hassan.
Post Box No. 121, BM Road, Hassan;
Ph: 08172-268731; www.hassanashok.com;
Tariff: ₹4,500–10,000 plus taxes.

HOTEL MAURYA VELAPURI, BELUR
This is a surprisingly clean and well-equipped facility by Karnataka State Tourism Department Corporation (KSTDC) if you want to make Belur the base camp for seeing all the temple sites. Very few people choose this option, considering Hassan has more options.
Temple Road, Belur; Ph: 08177-222209;
Tariff: ₹1,000–1,800 plus taxes.

HOYSALA VILLAGE RESORT, HASSAN
This is a good pick if you do not want to stay close to the touristy clutter. The suites are comfortable and clean, equipped with a kitchenette – perfect for an independence-loving tourist.
Belur Road; Ph: 08172-256764;
www.hoysalavillageresorts.in;
Tariff: ₹8,100–9,100 plus taxes.

SOUTHERN STAR, HASSAN
The spacious reception and polite staff immediately take the stress out of the busy traffic-clogged streets of Hassan. The rooms at Southern Star are clean and well equipped. A basic massage centre (8 a.m.–8 p.m.) can be booked in advance.
BM Road, Hassan; Ph: 08172-251816;
www.hotelsouthernstar.com;
Tariff: ₹4,400–5,500 plus taxes.

SUVARNA REGENCY, HASSAN
The hotel lies in the heart of the city, which makes it a convenient option. The rooms are spacious and clean, but the overall experience is pale if compared to other hotels. Choose Suvarna Regency for its location.
97, Bangalore–Mangalore Road;
Ph: 08172-264006;
www.suvarnaregencyhotel.com;
Tariff: ₹1,500 onwards plus taxes.

EATING OUT

THE ASHHOK HASSAN
The only restaurant in town where you can also order alcohol with your meals, Ashhok Hassan is also ideal for non-Indian cuisine.
Post Box No. 121, BM Road, Hassan;
Ph: 08172-268731; Timings: 12.30–10 p.m.;
Meal for 2: ₹500–1000.

HOTEL MAYURA SHANTHALA
Run by KSTDC, this is the only reasonable place to eat in Halebeedu. Close to the temple, the restaurant gets crowded during the season at lunchtime. Clean and safe to eat, Mayura is not a plush affair but serves both veg and non-veg food.
Near Temple, Halebeedu; Ph: 08177-273224;
Timings: 8.30 a.m.–9 p.m.;
Meal for 2: ₹250–500.

HOTEL MAYURA VELAPURI
Also run by the KSTDC, the restaurant is relatively new on the circuit. It serves basic but delicious food (veg and non-veg) in a clean environment. It lies close to the temple, so you need not allot too much time from your sightseeing hours.

Experience Karnataka

Temple Road, Belur; Ph: 08177-222209;
Timings: 10 a.m.–8 p.m.;
Meal for 2: ₹250–500.

HOTEL VISHNU REGENCY
Amongst the handful of options to eat here, choose this for vegetarian fare in a clean environment. Don't go in with high expectations, though.
KG Road, Belur; Ph: 09060982495;
Timings: 10 a.m.–8 p.m.;
Meal for 2: ₹250–500.

KARWAR
Part of the Southern Star hotel, the restaurant is ideal after a long day of sightseeing. Expect courteous staff, quick service and great pan-Indian food.
BM Road, Hassan; Ph: 08172-251816;
www.hotelsouthernstar.com; Timings:
12.30–10 p.m.; Meal for 2: ₹500–1,000.

SUVARNA
Although not high scoring on ambience and atmosphere, Suvarana — part of the Suvarna Regency Hotel — is great for a heavy south Indian meal.
97, Bengaluru–Mangaluru Road;
Ph: 08172-264006; Timings: 7 a.m.–10 p.m.;
Meal for 2: ₹250–500

DETOUR
Shravanabelagola

The poster picture of Karnataka with a massive statue of Bahubali, is Shravanabelagola's claim to fame. Though the town has no connect with the Hoysala trail, it is easy to club on the same route. This is a Jain pilgrimage, which will take about 4-5 hours, especially to see the

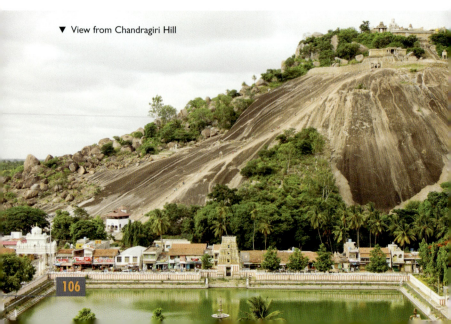

▼ View from Chandragiri Hill

Chandragiri and Vindhyagiri Hills. The towering Bahubali statue looms over the town from atop the Vindhyagiri Hill, which can be climbed from the *kalyani* (water body) side. The 57-feet tall monolithic statue of Lord Gomateshwara stands magnificently on top. Reach in time for the early morning prayers (8 a.m.) when devotees chant together.

> **TOP TIP**
> The hike on the rock-cut steps is not easy and should be avoided by elderly people. There are palanquins available for ₹200.

The largest draw of the place is the Mahamastakabhisheka, a festival celebrated every 12 years. On this day, the statue is bathed in consecrated water, milk, sugar cane juice and saffron paste. The next big day will be in 2018. On the opposite side of this hill are the older set of Jain temples on the Chandragiri Hill, which is easier to climb.

Sakleshpur

A pleasant alternative to the over-traversed coffee destinations of Karnataka, Sakleshpur offers a more low-key experience. Ever-pleasant weather, coffee-covered hills and spice plantations are the highlights. Plantation walks, luxury-estate stays and a credible base camp for the famous temple towns, Belur and Halebeedu, this adds some relief to the history-heavy trip.

Devotees sitting at the feet of Lord Gomateshwara

Experience Karnataka

The Manjarabad Fort was built by Tipu Sultan in 1792

One of the must-see places is Manjarabad Fort.

A weathered fort built by Tipu Sultan, as a strategic defense location is one of the few sightseeing interests here. Climb up the steep hill to get a bird's eye view of the entire region. Though unimpressive due to lack of upkeep or adequate information, the view makes up for the otherwise bland experience.

Betta Byreshwara is a 600-year-old temple that the spiritually inclined may find interesting. It is located at a short distance from Sakleshpur. Its historic value is ambiguous, but this, too, definitely provides a great view.

Nature lovers are sure to love the reserve forest area off the Bisle village. On a clear day, one can see the mountaintops of three adjoining regions: Kodagu, Hassan and south Karnataka. The rainforest region of The Bisle Reserve Forest is replete with birds and other wildlife. Visit only with local guides.

> **ALERT**: There is an alternative route to the steps, through the jungle, which is not recommended by locals.

ACCOMMODATION

THE HILLS
The Hills is one of the few luxury accommodations in Sakleshpur, the combination of Indonesian-style wooden cottages and luxury tents are well equipped and promise extreme comfort.
Kuntahalli Village, Devaladakere Post, Sakleshpur; Ph: 080-41158187; www.thehills.in; Tariff: ₹7,000–8,000 plus taxes.

JENKAL HOMESTAY
More than a century old, the home still retains its vintage charm with thick wooden pillars and an intricately carved door but offers all modern facilities. The Jenkal Homestay's great food and personal space will keep you coming back.
Near Devalankere, Sakleshpur; Ph: 09448144091; www.jenkal.in; Tariff: ₹4,500 plus taxes.

MUGILU
The view of the coffee estates bathed in mist from your balcony is the highlight of this homestay. Catch up on a good book, unwind and unplug from city life – that is the mantra of Mugilu.
Bugadahalli Village, Kyanahalli Post, Sakleshpur; Ph: 09845451055; www.mugilu.com; Tariff: ₹4,000 plus taxes.

THE PLANTERS BUNGALOW
The 7,500-acre Kadamane Tea Estate hosts guests in its century-old bungalow, which boasts illustrious ownership from the Earl of Warwick to tea conglomerate Brooke Bond. The English-styled house has high ceilings, a sprawling veranda and a marvellous view of tea-scapes. Great food, frequent elephant visits, treks in the property, and tea tasting are the highlights at The Planters Bungalow.
Kadamane Checkpost, Sakleshpur; Ph: 09481925930; www.sinnadorai.com; Tariff: ₹5,000 plus taxes.

EATING OUT

SURABHI'S NXT
Opt for Surabhi's Nxt for ample parking space, semi-open-air feel and a great view. Take a seat on the first floor to enjoy the view of coffee estates. The restaurant is slightly away from the town but the drive is worth the effort.
BM Road, Sakleshpur; Ph: 09008271807; Timings: 6 a.m.–10 p.m.; Meal for 2: ₹250–500.

SHOPPING

THE BEE KEEPERS CO-OPERATIVE SOCIETY LIMITED
Sakleshpur is famous for its freshly procured honey. A number of brands are available but you can buy from the Bee Keepers Co-operative.

The Coastal Route

Clouds gathering on Kapu Beach, Udipi

Mangaluru ▶ Udipi ▶ Jog Falls ▶ Gokarna ▶ Karwar

VITALS
Getting There
Mangaluru – earlier known as Mangalore – lies on the southwest edge of Karnataka, 353km west of Bengaluru. This is the base town to start one of the most stunning road trips along the west coast of Karnataka, right up north till Gokarna before Goa. The two major cities on this route are best connected by flight via Mangaluru airport (formerly Bajpe Airport). This is 9km from Mangaluru city and 53km from Udipi. Jet Airways, Spice Jet and Air India have frequent flights connecting major cities of India.

Mangaluru and Udipi both lie on the Konkan Railway belt and have ample trains from south Indian cities. From Bengaluru, there are three options, of which two trains run daily. Overnight buses by private and KSRTC (Karnataka State Road Transport Corporation) are a good option for an overnight ride of 9-10 hours. The entire stretch from Mangaluru to Karwar, with a detour to Agumbe and Jog Falls can be over 700km, a distance which can be traversed easily over a day's stop. It is recommended to also stay in Jog Falls for a night, so allocate time accordingly.

Best Time to Go
The cooler months from October to February are ideal for the coastal journey, except for the stop at Jog Falls. The full strength of the falls can be seen only in the monsoons or just after.

EXPLORING THE CIRCUIT

The Mangaluru–Gokarna stretch skirts the Arabian Sea for the greater part of the journey. The straight stretch is interjected by two spiritually inclined towns, Udipi and Murudeshwar. In-between, one also comes across the surfing village of Mulki, countless unknown beaches and two major pit stops of the Western Ghats: Agumbe Rainforest and Jog Falls. Any amount of superlatives falls pale for this part of Karnataka. Relatively unexplored, this route promises a raw landscape and travel ideas that are waiting to get pegged on itineraries.

Red-coloured tiled roofs, characteristic of Mangaluru, Udipi and places around (also known as Tulu Nadu) define the landscape of the region, throwing in splashes of copious greens with its lush forests and golden brown of the beaches. These are the three main colours that one encounters on the way. The area is an unexpected amalgamation of weathered temples, balmy sandy stretches and water sports luring tourists for an adventure-packed holiday. Apart from Kannada, Konkanese and a smattering of Hindi, the locals speak in Tulu, a Dravidian language that does not have its own script. What might strike you as unique and heart-warming, is the rich socio-cultural fabric of Mangaluru and surrounding areas, with a large presence of Hindus, Muslims and Christians living together.

Start this trip in Mangaluru, a city that is at the cusp of bursting into a fast-paced business centre,

▲ Baindur Beach, Udipi

Experience Karnataka

though firmly holding on to its easy-paced coastal life. This erstwhile 'beedi' capital of the country (there are many *beedi* factories here; *beedi* is an Indian cigarette) is now dotted with malls, shops, temples and colleges. Udipi, on the other hand, is imprinted as a Hindu pilgrimage site, with the famous Sri Krishna Math. With surfing and other water sports catching up as engaging activities, the region is not too far from exploding into a top destination for travellers, if they go right up the coast till Gokarna.

MANGALURU

SIGHTSEEING HIGHLIGHTS
Pilikula Nisargadhama

Less than 11km from the city, Pilikula Nisargadhama is a great stop if you are travelling with children. Start with the Biological Park, moving onto the Artisans' Village, a medicinal garden, Manasa Amusement Park and the Lake Garden. Potters at their wheels, cane and bamboo work and more indigenous crafts are the highlight of the Artisans' Village. The Manasa Amusement Park has water-specific rides (carry an extra pair of clothes and your own towels); however, do not expect very extensive paraphernalia. The best part of this complex is the Lake Garden and the boating options in the Pilikula (Tiger's) Lake. Self-pedalled boats are available to cruise on the scenic lake.

Mudushedde; Ph: 0824-226300; www.pilikula.com;

- **PILIKULA BIOLOGICAL PARK**
Entry Fee: Adults: ₹30, Children (between 6–12yrs.):₹15, Children (below 5 yrs.: ₹10; *Camera*: ₹25; *Video camera*: ₹100;
Timings: 9.30 a.m.–5.30 p.m.;

- **MANASA PARK**
Entry Fee: Adults: ₹250, Children: ₹170, Seniors: ₹150; *Video camera*: ₹100; *Camera*: ₹25;
Timings: 10.30 a.m.–5.30 p.m.;
Boating Charges: Adults: ₹10, Children: ₹5; *Video camera*: ₹100; *Camera*: ₹25; *Pedal 2/4 seater*: ₹100/120; *Motor boat*; ₹30.

> **TOP TIP**: Avoid weekends as the place is packed with local picnickers.

Someshwara Temple, dedicated to Lord Shiva, was built in the regime of Rani Abbakka Devi

Someshwara Beach and Temple

The Someshwara Temple of the town has one of the most scenic backdrops, with waves crashing onto its base. The Shiva temple is about 9km from Mangaluru, at the confluence of the Netravati River and the Arabian Sea, in Ullal. The temple was built under the regime of Rani Abbakka Devi, one of the first freedom fighters who resisted the Portuguese rule in the coastal region.

Timings: *6 a.m.–1 p.m., 3–8 p.m.*

Temple Trail of Mangaluru

The streets of Mangaluru are dotted with a number of Hindu temples, most of which are not particularly grand in architecture, but are very well known amongst the religiously inclined. You can spend an entire day on a temple trail, covering the most important ones. Of the many in the city, the ninth-century Mangaladevi

Impressive *gopurams* are a highlight of temples in southern India

Temple (**Timings**: 6 a.m.–1 p.m., 4–8.30 p.m.), Sharavu Mahaganapathi Temple (**Timings**: 6 a.m.–12.45 p.m., 4.15–8.45 p.m.), Urwa Marigudi (**Timings**: 6 a.m.–2 p.m., 4–8.30 p.m.), Venkataramana Temple on Car Street (**Timings**: 6.15 a.m.–1 p.m., 6–8 p.m.), the massive

Experience Karnataka

> **TOP TIP** Ensure that you slot mornings and evenings for temple sightseeing as all of them close for about 4 hours in the afternoon.

Kadri Manjunatheswara (**Timings**: 5 a.m.–1 p.m., 4–8 p.m.) and the elaborate Kudroli Gokarnanatheshwara (**Timings**: 6 a.m.–2 p.m., 4.30–9 p.m.) are the most visited ones. Most of the temples have a simple exterior with an intricate silver sanctum.

Cathedrals and Churches of Mangaluru

Christianity came into this part of the country with the Goan Catholics, making this a culturally rich region. The Rosario Cathedral, also known as Church of Our Lady of Rosary of Mangalore (Hampankatta; **Timings**: 9 a.m.–Noon, 3–7 p.m.) and the Milagres Church (Hampankatta; **Timings**: 6 a.m.–7 p.m.) are the two places that one should visit. The Rosario Cathedral, built in 1568, has an elaborate dome, and a cross, which lights up at night. Milagres, a Roman Catholic establishment, on the other hand, was built a whole century later by Bishop Thomas de Castro in 1680. The Italian missionaries played an important role in the development of the Mangalorean Catholic community and built the St Aloysius Chapel (**Timings**: 9.30 a.m.–6 p.m.; Sun: 8.30 a.m.–6 p.m.) in 1880. Go there to see the stunning paintings on the walls.

Rosario Cathedral, built in 1568

Ullal *dargah* commemorates the saint Seyyid Muhammad

Mosques
There are two important mosques that add to the wholesome religious topography of Mangaluru: the Seyyid Muhammad Shareeful Madani Dargah in Ullal (**Timings**: 5 a.m.–10 p.m.) and the Kudroli Jamia Masjid (Ph: 0824-2493133; www.kudrolijamiamasjid.com; Karbala Road, Kudroli; **Timings**: 5 a.m.–8.15 p.m.). The Ullal *dargah* (a shrine built over the remains of a Muslim religious figure) commemorates the saint Seyyid Muhammad who arrived here over 500 years ago, supposedly on a floating *chador* (prayer mat) that carried him across from Medina. The Urs festival here is held every five years with much zeal. The Kudroli Masjid is linked to the time of Tipu Sultan, as remnants of his rule in the form of a battery (watchtower) are close to this spot. Both mosques allow women inside.

Sultan Battery
In a derelict shape, this monument is a symbol of Tipu Sultan who constructed this watchtower in 1784 to look out for the British ships coming in through the Gurupura River behind it.

Seemanthi Bai Government Museum
Popularly known as the Bejai Museum, the city's official museum houses a number of coins, sculptures, remnants of British East India Company and paintings in neat exhibits.

Bejai Main Road, Mangaluru; **Entry Fee**: *₹2;* **Timings**: *10 a.m.–5 p.m., Mondays closed.*

DETOUR FOR A HISTORY LESSON IN JAINISM

The towns of Moodbidri (33km) and Karkala (50km) on NH13 make for a day-long detour to get oriented to the Jain influence in this region. The moniker of 'Jain Kashi' is attached to Moodbidri, a small town packed with Jain shrines, given that it is the seat of Digambara culture since AD 450. There are 18 important Jain temples here, of which the Thousand Pillar Basadi **(Timings**: 7 a.m.–6.30 p.m.) is the most important one. Over 600 years old, the architectural features of this temple are a mix of Oriental, Nepalese and Hoysala influences. The other *basadis* (temples) worth visiting are the Guru Basadi (commemorates Bhagwan Parshwanatha) and the Vikarama Shetty Basadi. There are 15 more around the region. You can take a break at the famous New Padivals Restaurant (Ph: 08258-236108; Near Old Police Station; **Timings**: 6 a.m.–10 p.m.; Meal for 2: Below ₹200) for south Indian snacks and meals.

Go further along 18km to Karkala to visit two important monuments on this Jain temple trail. Climb the well-constructed steps on a low granite hill to see the statue of Thyagaveera Bhagwan Shree Bahubali Swami **(Timings**: 9 a.m.–6 p.m.). The view of the green landscape of cashew and betel nut trees is gorgeous. You can also see the Chaturmukha Basadi **(Timings**: 9 a.m.–6 p.m.) on the opposite hill. This is more elaborate with the statues of Sri Adinath, Sri Mallinath and Sri Munisuvrat Nath in a dark sanctum. The temple was built in AD 1508 and has 108 intricately carved pillars. Inscriptions announce that the temple took thirty years to complete.

Chaturmukha Basadi, set amidst greenery

ACCOMMODATION

GINGER
This self-sufficient business hotel is clean and bright, a good option if you want to stay on the outskirts. Ginger has all modern amenities like an in-house restaurant, gym, Wi-fi and in-room dining. Good for a hassle-free stay.
Kottara Chowki Junction, Kuloor Ferry Road, Kottara; Ph: 1860266333; www.gingerhotels.com;
Tariff (incl. breakfast): ₹3,999.

GOLDFINCH
The most stylish boutique hotel in town, Goldfinch has pleasant interiors with modern facilities and great service. Discuss your room options with the staff while booking, as the double occupancy superior room can be pretty small. The hotel offers Wi-fi, a gym and a doctor on call.
Bunts Hostel Road; Ph: 0824-4245678;
www.goldfinchhotels.com;
Tariff (incl. breakfast): ₹3,950–15,000.

HOTEL DEEPA COMFORTS
The advantage of staying in Deepa Comforts is that you will be in the centre of the town, walking distance from the main business and shopping district. The rooms are reasonably comfortable and have Wi-fi, flat-screen TV and all other modern facilities in the room. There is also an in-house restaurant, in case you do not want to step out for meals.
MG Road, Ph: 0824-2497101;
www.hoteldeepacomforts.com;
Tariff (incl. breakfast): ₹2,950–4,750.

HOTEL PRESTIGE
The hotel offers great value for money, with the newly refurbished rooms on the fourth floor. Spacious, well lit, clean and with all modern facilities, the rooms also have Wi-fi.
Near Collectors Gate Balmatta Junction;
Ph: 0824-2410601; www.hotelprestige.in;
Tariff (incl. breakfast): ₹2,395–3,795.

THE OCEAN PEARL
Ocean Pearl's busy travel desk gives away that this is the most popular hotel in Mangaluru. Black-and-white photographs of the coastal region hang on the walls of the hotel and the aesthetics follow the rooms as well. Equipped with a soothing decor, well-lit spacious rooms and clean bathrooms, this is the top hotel in town. The hotel also offers free Wi-fi and facilities like gym, 24-hours' coffee shop, doctor on call and a lounge bar.
Navabharath Circle, Kodialbail; Ph: 0824-2413800;
www.theoceanpearl.in;
Tariff (incl. breakfast): ₹5,500–8,500.

PILIKULA NISARGHA DHAMA
The dowdy-looking building of Jungle Lodges has the most magnificent view of the Gurupura River; after all, the vantage location is the USP of Jungle Lodges. The accommodation is located in the scenic backdrop and close to the Manasa Amusement Park and the Pilikula Nisargha Dhama complex of zoo, artisans village, etc. Ask for a river-facing room.
Nisargadhama; Ph: 080-40554055;
www.junglelodges.com;
Tariff (incl. full board & entry fee to all Pilikula activities): ₹5,000–6,400.

THE SAFFRON
Though Saffron provides value for money, the rooms leave much to be desired in terms of being clean and bright. Stay here for proximity to the two main temples of the town (Car Street Venkataramana Temple and Kudroli Gokarnanatheshwara).
GHS Road, Hampankatta; Ph: 0824-4255542;
www.thesaffron.in;
Tariff (incl. breakfast): ₹2,999–4,999.

EATING OUT

BANASHRI HOTEL
The restaurant is a cosy, family savvy option for multi-cuisine dishes. Stick to the tasty Indian fare, especially the assortment of fish curries.
Tej Towers, 3rd Floor, Opp. Jyothi Cinema, Balmatta Road; Ph: 0824-2444929; www.pallkhi.com;
Timings: Noon–3 p.m., 7–11.15 p.m.;
Meal for 2: ₹250–500.

CORAL
The spacious and well-lit Coral at Ocean Pearl can be visited for a fine-dine experience with largely seafood delicacies and north Indian fare. For south Indian meals, visit Sagar Ratna (7 a.m.–11 p.m.) in the same hotel. The restaurants are local favourites, so be prepared to queue up for some time at meals.
Navabharath Circle, Kodialbail; Ph: 0824-2413800;
Timings: 11 a.m.–3.30 p.m., 6.30–11.30 p.m.;
Meal for 2: ₹250–500.

NEW TAJ MAHAL CAFÉ
A burst of conversation hits you as you enter this bustling snack joint, with regulars catching up over snacks and coffee.
Near Sankai Gudda Road; Ph: 0824-4269335;
Timings: 6 a.m.–10 p.m.; Meal for 2: Below ₹200.

SANADIGE
For a taste of typical Mangalorean cuisine, head straight to Sanadige at the Goldfinch hotel. If you are looking for a grill spread, Kabab Studio at the same hotel is also a good option.
Bunts Hostel Road, Near Jyoti Circle;
Ph: 0824-4245678; www.goldfinchhotels.com;
Timings: Noon–3.15 p.m., 7–11.15 p.m.;
Meal for 2: ₹250–500.

WOODLANDS
If you are an unfussy tourist, you will enjoy the quick but delicious meals at the no-frills, iconic 52-year-old Woodlands Hotel. Prepare to share tables with strangers, and be served on banana leaves.
Bunts Hostel Road; Ph: 0824-2443751;
Timings: 6 a.m.–9.45 p.m.; Meal for 2: Below ₹200.

SHOPPING

PHALGUNI CASHEW CENTRE
An assortment of dry fruits, especially cashews, is displayed temptingly at the town's best cashew stop. You can get a variety of them starting from ₹600/kg.
Shop No. 4, Hotel Roopa Bldg., Balmatta Road;
Ph: 0824-6566011; Timings: 8.30 a.m.–9.30 p.m.,
Sun: 9.30 a.m.–1.30 p.m.

TAJ MAHAL
Make your way to the small sweet shop in the heart of the city for a pack of sticky sweet Banana Halwa and toffee-like wrapped blobs of the delicious Badam Halwa.
Hampankatta; Ph: 0824-2421751;
Timings: 7 a.m.–9.30 p.m.

ALONG THE COAST

Ashram Surf Retreat, Mulki
There is no better place to learn or whet your skills other than the Ashram Surf Retreat in Mulki (22km) from Mangaluru. Camouflaged by dense greens, local homes and fields, it lies in the inconspicuous coastal village. The retreat is complemented by the Mantra Surf Club, which was established with a view to soak in yoga, meditation, simple veg food and, of course, riding the waves. Four simple double-occupancy rooms ensure that the group is an intimate one and the learning experience exclusive. Experts Jack Hebner and Rick Perry lead the team to help you manoeuvre surf breaks like Baba's Left and Swami and indulge in kayaking, body boarding, wake boarding and more.

- Mulki, Ph: 09880659130; www.surfingindia.net; Tariff (with full board, incl. yoga, day activities and Wi-fi): ₹3,500; surf equipment and lessons: ₹2,000 per head.
- Shaka Surf Club, along the coast, beyond Udipi, offers surf classes and the backdrop of a fishing village as well. Ph: 09820601985, 9986742710.

Mani, Udipi
Get in touch with Mani to try your hand at different aqua activities like banana boat rides, water scooter rides and a trip to the New Clean Island, 8km into the sea, off Udipi. On this trip, you can also expect to watch dolphins.

Ph: 09916773834; Cost: Water bike: ₹300, Banana boat: ₹200, Dolphin watching: ₹500.

Karavali Adventure, Udipi
Get in touch with Asif for guided para-sailing on the Malpe Beach. Weekends and holidays are packed with locals as well, so try and get hold of him on a lean day.

Ph: 074411559953; www.karavaliadventurs.com; Cost: Para-sailing: ₹500 per head.

Adreno
Between 15th June to 30th September, you can ride the rapids of Seethanadi with Adreno. Experience up to Grade 3 plus rapids here on stretches starting from 10–38km. You can choose from a few hours to overnight stay with the company.

57, 2nd cross, 7th C Main, RPC Layout Vijayanagar 2nd Stage, Bengaluru; Ph: 09448166970; www.adreno.org; Cost: Packages from ₹1,750–4,250.

Experience Karnataka

A day at Panambur Beach

Beaches Around Mangaluru

A large breezy stretch is the highlight of the town. Many of these beaches are just fishing villages with no infrastructure for tourists. Three beaches worth your while are the Tannir Bavi Beach (8km from the city), Panambur (10km from Mangaluru) and Surathkal (14km). Of these, Tannir Bavi has a huge parking area (₹20 for cars) and stone benches along the beach for you to sit and a few shops selling tea and snacks. Panambur, on the other hand, is action packed with plenty of snack shops, lifeguards, horse and camel rides and even some water sports facilities during October–February. Surathkal is famous for its NITK lighthouse (The lighthouse is off limits during the monsoon months).

Entry Fee: *Indians*: ₹10, *Children*: ₹3, *Foreigners*: ₹25; ***Camera***: ₹20; ***Video***: ₹25; ***Timings***: 4–5.30 p.m.

UDIPI

SIGHTSEEING HIGHLIGHTS
Sri Krishna Math

The thirteenth-century Krishna Temple is one of the key highlights of Udipi, with thousands snaking in a slow, long line along the temple pond for a brief moment to pay homage to the lord, whose idol can be seen only through a metal perforation. Built by the Vaishnavite saint, Sri Madhvacharya, the temple is cramped with devotees, especially during Janamashtami (Lord Krishna's birthday). There are a number of temples dating back to 1,500 years ago around this central attraction. The spacious Car Street stands parallel to the temple and is the entry point for the eight *mathas* that surround the temple.

Parking: ₹10; **Timings**: 5 a.m.–9.30 p.m.

Temples Around Udipi

In the decidedly Hindu social fabric of Udipi, you can be sure to see a temple at every bend. On the coastal stretch from Udipi to Murudeshwar, there are a number of temples that are worth your while. The Kunjarugiri Sri Durga Devi Temple (Ph: 0820-2559444; www.kunjarugiri.in; **Timings:** 7 a.m.–7.30 p.m.) lies south of the city on a low hill, overlooking the green countryside. The temple is believed to be established by Lord Parasurama, thousands of years

The awe-inspiring statue of Lord Shiva in Murudeshwar

Experience Karnataka

ago. Moving north of Udipi, the Anegudde Sri Vinayaka Temple in Kumbhashi (30km from Udipi; **Timings**: 6.30 a.m.–8.30 p.m.), Mookambika Devi Temple in Kollur (75km from Udipi, 40-km detour from Kundapura; **Timings**: 6 a.m.–1 p.m., 3 p.m.–8.30 p.m.) and Murudeshwar Temple (102km from Udipi; **Timings**: 6 a.m.–1 p.m., 3–8.30 p.m.) are the most important temples.

Mookambika Devi Temple lies on the banks of the Souparnika River, and holds great importance, as 1,200 years ago, Adi Shankara himself installed the idol here. The twenty-storeyed *gopuram* (gateway) of Murudeshwar Temple at the beachside town can be seen from afar. Make your way through a gate flanked by two life-size elephant sculptures to the sanctum on an elevated hillock on the left. You can also go up the lift up to the eighteenth floor of the *gopuram* for a spectacular view of the Arabian Sea all around. There is a park behind the temple, where a 123-feet statue of Shiva, overlooks the surrounding areas (**Timings**: 7 a.m.–7 p.m., Sat-Sun: 7 a.m.–9 p.m).

Coin Museum

The trajectory and evolution of Indian coins right from their inception to the latest launch can be traced in this unique coin museum, run by the Corporation Bank. Housed in founder, Khan Bahadur Haji Abdullah Haji Kasim Saheb Bahadur's house, coins and rupee notes right from 2,400 years ago can be seen here. Themed after various

The Coin Museum exhibits rare coins and currency notes from yesteryears

dynasties, colonial rule, independent India and commemorative coins, these are worthy collectibles. Mr MK Krishnayya guides visitors with enthusiasm, pointing out the various nuances and making them richer in the art of numismatics.

ALERT: Though the area is lush green and extremely beautiful in the rainy season, the water levels are alarmingly high.

PB No. 15, Corporation Bank Bldg.;
Ph: 0820-2530955;
Timings: *10 a.m.–5 p.m.*

Museum of Anatomy and Pathology

More than forty years old, this museum is an excellent repertoire of hundreds of specimens of human and animal anatomy. Extremely well maintained, the Museum of Anatomy and Pathology houses human and animal organs, apart from some bizarre biological exhibits.

Manipal; **Entry Fee***: Adults: ₹10,*
Children: ₹5; **Timings***: 8 a.m.–5 p.m.*

Jomlu Theertha Falls

A 30-km drive from Udipi, through a shaded, forested path flanked by cashew trees and dense undergrowth, takes you to the Jomlu Theertha Falls. The 20-feet waterfalls on the Sita River are a popular hotspot, so avoid weekends. For closer access to the falls, it's best to go in the non-monsoon months.

Beaches Around Udipi

A number of fishing villages and small towns dot the coastal stretch from Udipi to Murudeshwar. Many of the beaches are not developed for tourism and pleasantly retain the fishing culture. Closer to Udipi, Kaup (15km; locally called Kapu) is tourist savvy with a few shops and the towering lighthouse that is the key attraction (**Entry Fee**: ₹10; **Timings**: 4–6 p.m.; closed in monsoons). Mattu Beach (8.5km south of Udipi) is a quiet spot, not plagued by the surge of tourists. Malpe (8km) is a bustling local tourist spot with horse and camel rides, small food stalls and

Mattu Beach, serene and calm, is a perfect getaway ▶

Murudeshwar Beach, a perfect landscape

These beaches make for brilliant stops along the route but are unsafe for swimming.

even water sports (Ph: 7411559953; www.karavaliadventures.com; **Cost**: para-sailing ₹500 per head) in non-monsoon months.

Another prominent stop by the highway is the Maravanthe Beach (53km). This is especially scenic as the highway is flanked on either side by the beach and the Souparnika River. You can halt at the Turtle Bay Resort (www.turtlebayeco.com) for a meal. The Baindur Beach is a dramatic rocky outcrop. Follow the hillside along the beach and get a better viewing spot from the top. Here, you can make a stop at Sai Vishram Resort (Ph: 08254-323902; www.saivishram.com). In Murudeshwar, the popular tourist beach, you can stop at RNS Residency (Ph: 08365-268901; www.naveenhotels.com), which commands a vantage spot by the sea and is a stone's throw away from the temple.

St Mary's Island

Off the Malpe coast, the non-monsoon months allow you to take a short excursion, 3km into the sea where you can visit a cluster of islands – Dari Bahadur Garh, Coconut Island, South Island and North Island. Together, these are called St Mary's Islands, formed by basaltic lava. The best time to visit is between December to March (Ph: 09740981755; **Cost**: ₹100–150 to visit one island, pay more to visit all; **Timings**: 8 a.m.–5 p.m.).

ACCOMMODATION

BLUE MATSYA
A pleasant respite for tourists who just want to kick off their shoes and dig their toes in the sand, Blue Matsya is blissfully elusive, though just off the Lighthouse at Kaup Beach. The white-walled home, dotted with blue windows is a self-catering beach house. Brightly furbished, its two rooms on different floors gives you ample privacy, but you also have help close at hand; Ramanna, the caretaker, lives just next door. A well thought-out instruction guide by the owner, Swati, equips you to have a great time. Though the house is extremely comfortable, you are likely to be spending most of the time in the balconies for the view of the waves lashing at the lighthouse in the distance.
Lighthouse Road, Kaup Beach; Ph: 09820770427; www.bluematsya.com;
Tariff: ₹3,800–5,000 (minimum 2 nights).

DIANA
A time-tested establishment, everyone in Udipi will ask you to visit the Diana restaurant for the famous ice cream called 'Gadbad'. The new address of the restaurant also has a spanking new set of rooms; much cleaner and spacious than most in the city. This is also close to the temple.
Near Big Bazar, Jodukatte, Ajjarkad; Ph: 0820-2520505; Tariff (incl. breakfast): ₹2,000–2,200.

FORTUNE INN VALLEY VIEW
One of the best options in Manipal and Udipi both, the Fortune hotel provides options for in-house dining and well-decorated, comfortable rooms and lies in the middle of Manipal city.
PB No. 174, Manipal; Ph: 0820-2571101; www.fortunehotels.in;
Tariff (incl. breakfast): ₹6,000–11,000.

PALM GROVE BEACH RESORT
If you are looking to stay at a secluded spot on the beach, Yermal's Palm Grove is a simple but tasteful option. More so, it's right on the beach. The resort lies adjacent to a fishing village. Watching the catch come in the morning is the most exciting activity here.
Fisheries Road, Yermalbada, Ph: 09008444891;
Tariff (incl. breakfast): ₹2,500.

PARADISE ISLE
One of the oldest hotels of the area, stay in Paradise Isle for its proximity to the beach and excellent service. The rooms are old and musty but this is your best bet to stay right on the beachfront.
Malpe; Ph: 0820-2538666; www.theparadiseisle.com;
Tariff (incl. breakfast): ₹3,500–8,500.

SAI RADHA HERITAGE
A cosy unit of four rooms in a traditional house, a beach-facing three-roomed complex and a single room make the stay arrangement at Sai Radha Heritage. Aimed at Ayurveda enthusiasts, this is ideal for long-stay guests. Book ahead if you want to ensure that you get a room of your choice. The rich Indian aesthetics, traditional decor and great food makes for a soothing experience.
Behind Muloor Panchayat, Bikriguthu Road, Muloor; Ph: 09243350458; www.sairadhaheritage.com;
Tariff (incl. breakfast): ₹3,000–5,000.

WILD WOODS SPA
Though Wild Woods is 85km from Udipi, if you are doing the coastal stretch, this secretive spot is a delight. It sits along a stream and can be reached through a drive between bamboo clusters and the forest. The resort lies 6km off the highway but is worth your while for its intimate cottages, well-versed naturalists, excellent Ayurveda facilities and plenty of outdoor activities.
Shiroor, Check Post Deviation, Toodahalli Village, Yadthare Panchayat, Kundapur; Ph: 08254-250666; www.wildwoodsspa.com; Tariff (incl. full board & additional activities): ₹5,500–6,500.

EATING OUT

The region is replete with several options of cuisines but what you will really want to dig your teeth in, is the coastal cuisine. Don't leave without trying the iconic Sol Kadi, a coconut milk and kokum beverage, known for its digestive properties.

MITRA SAMAJ
This is a symbol of Udipi's famous south Indian cuisine. Mitra Samaj is the busiest place in town with crisp dosas making their way through packed tables at breakneck speed. It lies on the wide Car Street, next to the Sri Krishna Temple.
Car Street; Ph: 0820-2520502;
Timings: 5.30 a.m.–9.30 p.m., Wednesdays closed; Meal for 2: ₹250–500.

SAROVAR
For vegetarian multi-cuisine fare, Sarovar is a decent option between the middle of the city and Malpe. The restaurant is spacious and has a separate AC section.
Karvali Bypass; Ph: 0820-2529145;
Timings: 7 a.m.–11 p.m.; Meal for 2: ₹250–500.

THAAMBOOLAM
A bullock cart, indigenous wall designs and more make for great decor and a pleasing ambience at Thaamboolam. The brilliant food (especially the fish) will ensure that you have a fulfilling meal here.
Opp. Kalpana Theatre, Comfort Tower;
Ph: 0820-4296418; Timings: 10.30 a.m.–3.30 p.m., 6.30–11.30 p.m.; Meal for 2: ₹250–500.

THONSEPAR
Malpe's only claim to a beachside shack, Thonsepar, a little café near the parking section is a relaxing spot for an evening coffee and snacks. The café also has a few rooms right at the beachfront (₹1,500–2,500).
Malpe Beach; Ph: 09902009595;
Timings: 10 a.m.–8 p.m.; Meal for 2: Below ₹200.

WOODLANDS
One of the oldest establishments in town, you can get the most authentic Udipi dosa at Woodlands, along with a reasonable spread of north and south Indian dishes. The dingy basement restaurant gets packed during lunchtime with devotees visiting the Krishna Temple (it's a short distance away).
Dr UR Rao Complex, Near Sri Krishna Math, Thenkapet;
Ph: 0820-2522807; Timings: 8.30 a.m.–3.30 p.m., 5.30–10.30 p.m.; Meal for 2: Below ₹200.

SHOPPING

AIRODY RADHAKRISHNA PAI & SONS
When visiting Udipi, you are likely to be inducted into the religious zeal of the town. For religious souvenirs like **metal statues**, **incense stick holders** and **metal pots**, visit Airody Radhakrishna Pai & Sons.
Car Street; Ph: 0820-2520957; Timings: 8 a.m.–1 p.m., 3–8 p.m., Sundays closed.

DETOUR
Agumbe

A 650-metre high rainforest plateau, with many monikers to its credit – 'Capital of King Cobra', 'Home to Malgudi Days' and 'Cherrapunji of the South' – a trip to Agumbe packs in diverse experiences. It lies 55km northeast of Udipi, through a breathtaking forested path. A world heritage site and one of the wettest parts of the Western Ghats (rainfall of at least 8,000mm for five months), Agumbe is a biodiversity hotspot, specifically known for its King Cobra population and other rare amphibians and reptiles.

STAY AND DO

- Know more about the land of the deadliest snake in the world at renowned herpetologist P Gowri Shankar's Camp, about 7km from Agumbe village. Stay in tented accommodation in the 5-acre property and immerse yourself in nature. You can just soak in the thickly green environs or attend well-constructed workshops/camps that acquaint you with much dreaded creatures, snakes!

Kalinga Mane, Churrchihakklu, Agumbe Hobli, Hosur Grama, Guddekere, Shimoga, Ph: 09986291641; Tariff (double tent, incl. full board & activities): ₹2,000; 3-day Herp Camp: ₹2,500 per day/per head.

▼ Verdant Agumbe offers interesting experiences to nature lovers

Experience **Karnataka**

MAJOR ART FORMS AND FESTIVALS OF COASTAL KARNATAKA

Coastal Karnataka is rife with ancient traditions and festivals of which Bhutha Kola and Yakshagana performances, and the Kambala buffalo races are most famous. Apart from these, betting on cockfights in villages and Pulikkali (Tiger Dance) are also important cultural events. There is no specific calendar for these activities, and one has to depend on local knowledge, posters and local newspaper announcements for finding out the venues of these performances.

- **Kambala (Buffalo Race)**: Over 1,000 years old, the tradition of racing buffaloes in water-filled tracks still evokes massive excitement in the villages, though the festival has come under fire for cruelty to animals. Originally a farmer's sport, the races were later patronized by kings. Over 45 *kambalas* (buffalo races) are held from November until March. Of these, the Kadri Kambala in Mangaluru is the most famous, but the ones in villages are less commercial and give you a more authentic insight. Since there is no fixed calendar for these events, one is highly dependent on local knowledge. The races are a two-day affair, continuing overnight as well.

- Another pit stop in the heart of the forested regions of Agumbe is the government-run Seethanadi Nature Camp. Tented accommodation, nature trails and River Sita flowing right next to the camp are the highlights here.

Hebri Village, Ph: 09480807650; Tariff (double tent, incl. food): ₹1,500.

- Visit Kasturi Akka's home, Dodda Mane in Agumbe. The claim to fame of this large, century-old house is that two episodes of the legendary TV serial *Malgudi Days* were shot here in 1985. A family of eight still live in the house and entertain guests. The family, however, is happy to host hundreds of guests over a month and feed them meals at no cost. It is recommended to offer anything that you desire (Ph: 08181-233075).

- Agumbe can be used as a base to cover a number of picturesque waterfalls like Jogi Gundi, Onake Abbi, Barkana, Kundadri and Koodlu Theertha. One has to walk anywhere between ½km to 6km to reach these, so avoid going there in monsoons. The paths are ridden with leeches.

- A further detour of 28km from Agumbe, and you can reach the famous Dakshinamnaya Sri Sharada Peetham at Sringeri. The *peetham* also received patronage from the Vijayanagar Empire followed by a number of dynasties and rulers who were drawn to this seat of learning for the Sanatana Dharma. You can visit the temple here and also eat a simple free community meal.

Ph: 08265-250123;
www.sringerisharadapeetham.org; Timings: 6 a.m.–2 p.m., 4–9 p.m.; Meal timings: 12.15–2.30 p.m., 7.15–8.30 p.m.

JOG FALLS

A monsoon special on the Western Ghats, Jog Falls' Raja, Rani, Roarer and Rocket waterfalls plunge down from a height of 830 feet, earning the group a second place in the legacy of one of the highest waterfalls of Asia. The falls lie on the Sharavathi River and create a magical haze of spray for those who brave proximity, down the steps to the base. There are two ways to see Jog Falls (also known as Gerusoppa Falls) – one from Shimoga district and the other from Karwar, just a few kilometres ahead. While the Shimoga (more popular side) is the point from where you see all four waterfalls together, the Karwar side has the closest access.

The Rocket Waterfall, one of the cascades at Jog Falls, is a major tourist attraction

The main entry point is better organized with 1,500 steps leading down to the base of the falls. The stone steps have proper railings and unlike old times – when the path was not so well paved – the steep downhill climb is not too hard on the legs. You can get as close as 30 metres from the base of the falls and enjoy the spray. As expected, this is the most trigger-happy place in Jog Falls.

Entry Fee: Adults: ₹5, Children: ₹5; **2-wheelers**: ₹10, **4-wheelers**: ₹30; **Timings**: 7 a.m.–7 p.m.

SIGHTSEEING HIGHLIGHTS
Muppane

A forested area that leads to a wide expanse of backwaters of the Sharavathi River, Muppane is one of those wonderfully elusive spots that the offbeat tourist will love. You have to drive 3km inside the forest to reach this spot. From the edge, you can see a number of small islands, which can only be accessed by a boat. Get in touch with Sampath (Ph: 09663585591), who organizes boating here.

(**Cost**: ₹300 per ride; **Timings**: 8.30 a.m.–5 p.m.).

▼ Muppane, a forested area, by the Sharavathi River

Keladi Temple

Built in the Dravidian style with inspiration from Hoysala architecture, the ancient Keladi Temple lies 31km from Jog Falls. The main attraction here is the weathered but intricately carved sculptured walls of the Rameshwara and Veerabhadra temples.

Timings: 8 a.m.–9 p.m.

Keladi Museum

Step in to know more about the Keladi Nayakas through well-kept exhibits and a guide that tells you more about the Keladi dynasty. Artefacts, objects of common use, manuscripts on palm leaves and large sculptures span out a brief history of the ruling kings in the medieval period. The key attraction here is a large wooden chariot inside a room outside the museum. It belongs to the Ikkeri Temple close by.

Timings: 10 a.m.–5 p.m.

Kalasi

The twin Shiva temples in Kalasi lie 38km from Jog Falls. The Lord Neelakanteshwara Temple and Lord Mallikarjuna Temple were built in the twelfth century in Hoysala-style of architecture. This is still an active temple with a large Nandi outside the Mallikarjuna Temple.

Timings: 6 a.m.–8 p.m.

The Kalasi Temple surrounded by greenery

Experience Karnataka

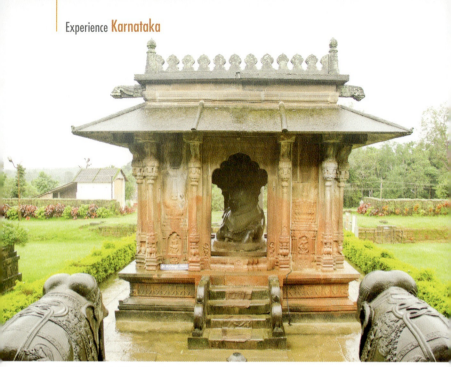

Nandi shrine in Ikkeri Temple

Ikkeri

The erstwhile capital of the Keladi Nayakas, Ikkeri, houses a grand reminder of the rulers between AD 1540 and 1640 – the Aghoreshwara (Shiva) Temple. The large, carved columns of the temple with a massive Nandi in front adds to the grandeur of the Hoysala and Kadamba architecture along with other features such as a highly ornate doorway, old Kannada manuscripts and the sculptures of the 32 female figures called Shakti Peetha.

Timings: 7 a.m.–1.30 p.m., 4.30–7.30 p.m.

Gerusoppa, a Jain heritage centre

Gerusoppa

This is Jain heritage centre, which developed in the 13th–16th centuries. A forested path leads to the Jain complex with the main attraction as the Chaturmukha Basadi. It is said that the ruins of the place comprised 108 temples in a 700-acre surrounding region, but now only a handful are distinctly visible. Apart from the main *basadi*, Sri Parshwanatha Basadi, Sri Mahavir Temple and Sri Neminath Temple can also be seen.

Timings: 6 a.m.–8 p.m.

Gudavi Bird Sanctuary

The Gudavi Bird Sanctuary is a delight to visit for the scenic ride through Sorab town. The 182-acre sanctuary is surrounded by a moat in some parts and has two towers and a cemented path to walk around. Small jetties off the main path are good viewing pads to see birds like the grey heron, jungle fowl, waterfowl, Indian pond heron, cormorants, white Ibis, the Indian shag and more. The best time to visit here are September and October when the population is much more.

Entry Fee: *Indians: ₹50, Foreigners: ₹300;*
Timings: *9 a.m.–6.30 p.m.*

Gudavi Bird Sanctuary attracts a wide variety of birds

ACCOMMODATION

GUNDIMANE
Located between a 100-acre plantation of areca trees, coffee, pepper and fruits, Mrs Chandrakala and Mr Ganapathi Rao's home is the most authentic homestay experience that you can get in this region. They have opened the four first-floor rooms of their house for guests who would like to have a peaceful tryst with nature. The best part of the home is the common balcony where guests meet for meals. It looks out to a large hill in front of the house where bison and deer sighting is common.
Gundimane Aralgodu; Ph: 09900956760; www.gundimane.com; Tariff (double occupancy, excl. meals): ₹1,700.

KSTDC HOTELS
The well-maintained 'Sharavathi' block of the KSTDC hotels inside the Jog Falls complex is one of the most popular picks for travellers. Pick the first-floor rooms for better view of the falls. The smaller 'Tunga' block is aimed at backpackers and can be avoided. All bookings are to be done online.
Jog Falls; Sharavathi Block; Ph: 0818-6244732; www.karnatakaholidays.net; Tariff: ₹1,800 (double occupancy, non-AC), ₹2,200 (AC), Tunga Block: ₹800 (non-AC), ₹1,800 (dormitory, 10 beds).

MATTHUGA
There are two accommodation types that you can choose from – spacious but sparse four rooms in the main house or individual twin cottages between the property's areca plantations. The rooms are clean, spacious and economical but if you are travelling with family, you may want to use the larger twin rooms in cottages. The food served here is home-made and vegetarian.
Talavata (Near Jog Falls), BH Road (NH206); Ph: 09880799975; www.matthuga.in; Tariff (incl. breakfast): ₹1,700, Cottages: ₹2,600.

EATING OUT

There aren't too many restaurants in Jog Falls, so most travellers stick to meals at the accommodation where they are staying. The only decent place to eat is the KSTDC restaurant in the Jog Falls complex (Timings: 7 a.m.–7 p.m.), which serves multi-cuisine fare.

GOKARNA

SIGHTSEEING HIGHLIGHTS
Beaches of Gokarna

Once a quiet spot for evening strolls, Gokarna Beach now performs the function of a bathing spot for the devotees entering the Mahabaleshwar Temple. As a result, the beach is not secluded any more.

Om Beach, where two semicircular coves join in the middle, making a natural 'Om', is still the most popular beach of the town. Though you cannot find pristine sandy swathes or aqua marine water, the hillocks surrounding the beach and the simple shacks dotting the stretch are the highlight here. (Distance: 4km from main Gokarna town; **auto rickshaw fare**: ₹250).

For One Tree Point, walk up the dirt trail towards the cliff from Dolphin Shanti Café at the end of Om Beach, and you will find the path that goes towards Half Moon Beach. As you pass through a rocky divide, casuarina trees and wild thorn bushes to climb higher, the view of the sea below will get more spectacular. Ten minutes into the hike (20-minute trek from Om Beach), you will find one lone tree standing on the cliff that juts into the sea. From here, one can see the holy shape of Om.

Kudle Beach is easily a 20-minute trek on a treacherous

Gokarna is known for its beautiful beaches ▼

Experience Karnataka

TOP TIP: Foreigners are not allowed; men allowed only if bare-chested.

footpath from Om Beach. Kudle gets a smaller share of the beach goers and is populated more by people who live long term in its numerous guesthouses and shacks. This clean, 1-km stretch of beach is dotted with sunbathers, volleyball players and shacks jostling with each other for space – but only during the winter season. For the rest of the year, the place looks derelict (20-minutes trek from Om to Kudle Beach; **auto rickshaw fare**: ₹80).

More of a cove than a beach, Half Moon Beach is somewhat of a hideout, away from the clutter. After you finish the long trek from Om Beach to Half Moon Beach, you may be disappointed by the sight of this small strip of rocky sand flanked by hillocks on both sides. But for those who like to be isolated, this is splendid (**boat fare** to Half Moon Beach: ₹300 per head).

In Paradise Beach, once believed to be a nudist beach and the party capital of the hippies, it's difficult to get the same vibe here. With construction work around the beach, it wears an abandoned look. Paradise Beach can be reached by foot, but the trek is a tad difficult (**boat fare**: ₹300 per head).

Shops on Temple Street

Mahabaleshwar Temple

There are three parts of this famous Shiva shrine. First is the Sree Tamra Gowri Temple, dedicated to Shiva's consort, Parvathi, who is also known as Swayamvar Parvathi in this temple.

The Maha Ganapathy Shrine stands just outside the Mahabaleshwar Temple, to honour Ganapathy as a small boy who deceived Ravana and embedded the Shivlinga in Gokarna. (**Entry Fee**: ₹1; **Timings**: 5.30 a.m.–12.30 p.m., 5–9 p.m.). Koti Theertha, a large man-made pond close to the temple, is used for holy baths and immersion of idols. But the main shrine is that of the irregular shaped *atmalingam* (self-manifested, or created on it's own) protruding only a few inches from the ground. This is encased on the flower and is often doused with milk, *ghee* (clarified butter), flowers and offerings, so one cannot see the *lingam*.

Timings: 6 a.m.–12.30 p.m., 5–8 p.m.

Mirjan Fort

Eleven kilometres from Gokarna lies a well-preserved fort, an erstwhile port for the trade of spices, most importantly pepper, which earned its queen – Chennabhairavi Devi Gerusoppa – the moniker of Pepper Queen. Built in the 1600s under both Portuguese and Islamic influences, Mirjan Fort had living quarters, an audience hall, functioning kitchens and elaborate waterworks, most of which still stand strong and make one travel to the 1600s seamlessly.

Timings: Sunrise to Sunset.

Yana Rocks

It's worth keeping a full day aside for the extraordinary sight of gigantic black rock formations shooting out from the middle of a dense forest, just 40km from Gokarna on the Sirsi Road. An hour's drive from Gokarna, the Yana Rocks are located in the middle of a dense forest. From the car park, walk for over an hour in the silent, cool forest. At the end of this hike, and about 250 steps away, you will be rewarded by the sight of Bhairaveshwara Shikara and Mohini Shikara, two black, limestone rocks that house secret temples in their caves.

ACCOMMODATION

GOKARNA INTERNATIONAL
In Gokarna, you might have to choose between staying with an attached bathroom or staying by the sea. Here, there is no dilemma. At Gokarna International, you get both. The odd, concrete building among a line of basic beach shacks, this hotel offers a great view of the sea, and has kept true to its Gokarna roots by offering a shack as its restaurant.
Kudle Beach; Ph: 08884741005; Tariff (double occupancy): ₹2,000.

HOTEL ASHOKAVANA
Ashokavana is pleasantly away from the touristy clutter, yet not too far from the temple (₹20 by auto). The rooms are very spacious and clean. The hotel also has an in-house 24-hours' café, so you do not have to step out for food each time.
Melinakeri, IB Road, Gokarna; Ph: 08386-257048; www.ashokavana.com; Tariff (double occupancy): ₹1,800–2,300.

HOTEL SHRI SAI RAM
One of the cleanest options on the busy main road near the temple, do not go by the entrance of Shri Sai Ram. The rooms are clean and have better facilities like TV and AC, which are not offered by many other guesthouses.

Main Road, Ganjigadde, Near Bus Stand; Ph: 08386-257755; Tariff (double occupancy): ₹500–1,300.

JJK RESORT
A bit of a misfit in the boho world of Gokarna, this resort offers a king-sized bed, 32-inch plasma TV with the Arabian Sea laid out like a carpet in front.
Kudle Beach; Ph: 09620884136; Tariff (double occupancy): ₹3,000.

KHUSHI VILLAGE
The one thing going for this place is the location. Nestled in a grove in the middle of a forest, it is suited more to the rugged nature lover.
Om Beach Road, Niralla; Ph: 8386257903; www.khushivillageresorts.com; Tariff (double occupancy): ₹1,200.

LINGER
Promoting 'do nothing' vacations, Linger keeps the promise in Gokarna, by offering a great place to relax and be one with nature, and unplug from city life. The rustic feel of the place and a definite eco-inclination is appreciated by those who are conscious tourists.
Bavikodla; Ph: 09590050001; www.linger.in; Tariff: Packages ₹4,950 onwards.

NAMASTE CAFÉ & NAMASTE YOGA FARM
This most famous guesthouse at Om Beach offers the quintessential Gokarna experience — beer, a convenience store, a tattoo studio, Internet services and Ayurvedic massages. If yoga is more your thing, then head to Namaste Yoga Farm on a hillock above Kudle Beach — this is more low key.
Om Beach; Ph: 08386-257141; Tariff (double occupancy): ₹900–1,500.

NIRVANA CAFÉ
Colourful kitschy artwork on the huts, scattered in a small grove, are usually booked out soon. It is the liveliest place in the evenings and offers a glorious sunset in its big, clean, beachfront café, where you can sip your coffee with toes dug deep in the sand.
Om Beach; Ph: 9742466481; Tariff (double occupancy): ₹500.

OM BEACH RESORT
One of the only 'resort' options in Gokarna, Om Beach Resort sits at a distance from the chaos of the beach. The rooms are simply furnished but are big and come with balconies. If you want to pass up the gastronomic delights of Gokarna and eat all your meals here, this could make for a great family holiday destination.
Om Beach Road; Ph: 8386257052; www.ombeachresorts.com; Tariff (double occupancy; incl. all meals): ₹6,000.

SHASTRI GUEST HOUSE
The main building of the Shastri Guest House cannot be seen from the main road, so it is difficult to imagine the 60-roomed building with numerous options of rooms. The rooms are bare, with no modern facilities, but are comfortable enough for a night's stay.
Near Bus Stand; Ph: 08386-256220; Tariff (double occupancy): ₹300–600.

ZOSTEL
New on the hospitality scape of Gokarna, Zostel carries the baton of the first hostel option in the coastal town. You will not be disappointed — cheap rooms, great views and excellent company converge here.
Kudle Beach Road; Ph: 09535340446; www.zostel.com; Tariff (dorm. to private room): ₹599–1,799.

EATING OUT

ARYA
The temple of health food in Gokarna, Arya operates one of the cleanest open kitchens in this area, where you can oversee the preparation of simple but delicious vegetarian meals, based on Ayurveda concepts. Try the Pumpkin Curry (₹70) with organic rice and Puttu (steamed dumpling). Don't leave without picking up a few of their pure oils from the cash counter.
Kudle Beach; Ph: 9341254771;
Timings: 8 a.m.–10 p.m.; Meal for 2: ₹500–750.

DOLPHIN BAY CAFÉ
'Hello to the King, Hello to the Queen, Bhagsu with ice cream' at the Dolphin Bay Café, is no weird refrain, but menu specials at Dolphin! Located right in the middle of the beach, across the rocky outcrop which gives Om Beach its shape, the Dolphin Bay Café is hard to miss. 'Hello to the King' (₹115), a uniquely Gokarna concoction of ice cream, cake and Parle biscuits, is a must-try.
Om Beach; Timings: 8 a.m.–11 p.m.;
Meal for 2: ₹500–750.

DRAGON CAFÉ
A legacy of great wood-fired oven pizzas await you at Dragon Café. There are at least twenty different varieties of pizza here — Seafood Pizza (₹180), Cheese Egg Pizza (₹140) and more.
Kudle Beach; Timings: 8 a.m.–11 p.m.;
Meal for 2: ₹500–750.

JAZZMIN CAFÉ
Six lovely cane chairs sitting under a tree on a beach-facing patio make for the seating at Jazzmin Café — and who wouldn't be enticed with such a setting. Open all day, you can find it simply by seeing the large Shiva mural on its main wall. Try the home-made bread, Cinnamon Rolls, Ginger Honey Lime Tea (₹20) for a breakfast that's light on the tummy and the pocket as well.
Kudle Beach; Timings: 8 a.m.–11 p.m.;
Meal for 2: ₹500–750.

NAMASTE CAFÉ
Fully loaded breakfast options from different countries, all-day-long beer and great Indian cuisine is what one can expect in Namaste. Getting a cup of tea and staring into the sea is also an option.
Om Beach; Ph: 08386-257141;
Timings: 8 a.m.–11 p.m.; Meal for 2: ₹500–750.

OM SHANTI CAFÉ
Om Shanti is a big, clean shack with splendid wall art on its huts and astonishingly a menu card that spells correctly! The Spinach Mushroom Pasta (₹75) or Calamari Macaroni (₹85) are an excellent choice.
Om Beach; Timings: 8 a.m.–11 p.m.;
Meal for 2: ₹250–500.

PAI HOTEL
Close to the Venkataramana Temple, a small, bright, yellow-walled café dishes out the best south Indian treats in town, including Kesar Pedas. This is the only place on the street worth a stop for a meal. There is another 'Pai' establishment on the same street with similar cost and aesthetics.
Car Street (close to the Venkataramana Temple);
Timings: 6 a.m.–8 p.m.; Meal for 2: ₹500.

Experience Karnataka

KARWAR

SIGHTSEEING HIGHLIGHTS
Karwar Beach
Karwar Beach is the single-most important highlight of the town. This isn't a beach where you can soak up the sun and relax with a chilled beer. Instead, this is the beach which is great to roam with children and stop at its myriad attractions en route – the fantastic warship museum with its life-sized replica of the *INS Chapal*, or the aquarium.

The Warship Museum, is on the main beach road.

Entry Fee: ₹15; *Timings*: 10 a.m.–7.30 p.m.; *a musical fountain plays from 7–7.30 p.m. every evening.*

Lighthouse Island
Built in 1679, the Oyster Rock Lighthouse stands in magnificent isolation on an island, more like a speck of red in the blue sea. With its polished brass fittings, teak wood cabinets and wrought-iron railings, it's more like a relic, but does throw light upon things like Global Positioning Systems. If that interests you, do not leave this highlight. It's located 8km off the coast of Karwar (**boat fare**: ₹1,500 for a return trip).

Kurumgad Island
The 45-minute boat ride to Kurumgad Island is worth your time but only in the morning, before the sun has had a chance to turn the island into a scalding rock in the middle of the ocean. It is rife with birds, flora and fauna, which you will discover during your nature walk.

Ph: 08382-594574; Great Outdoors offers a nature walk at 8 a.m.; **Cost**: *₹500, including pick up and drop.*

Devbagh Beach
Devbagh Beach is not easy to get to, as it's a combination of an island and a beach, and can be accessed only by boat that runs on a fixed-time schedule. But once you manage to get there, the trouble is worth it. No crowds, shady copse, sand, hammocks and sun – you get the picture.

Ph: 08382-226596; Jungle Lodges runs a boat service to Devbagh Beach all through the day; **Cost**: *₹200 per head; Contact their office, just after Karli Bridge.*

Majali Beach
The fishing village of Majali does not hold the touristy draw of Devbagh, but is an incredibly beautiful strip of beach that off-beat travellers will love. The Devbagh–Majali 5-km stretch runs parallel to NH17.

ACCOMMODATION

DEVBAGH BEACH RESORT
One of the most popular resorts in the area, Devbagh has managed the feat of being the only one on an incredible stretch of sand. The resort has log cabins and cottages that are large, but minus the frills. The prices are high. The restaurant has buffet meals and the resort offers water sports.
Devbagh Beach, Kodibagh; Ph: 08021-2444444; www.devbaghbeachresort.com; Tariff (incl. all meals): ₹4,000.

EMERALD BAY
Overlooking the Kali River, Emerald Bay shines in comparison to the other more rugged options in the area, since it is the only high-end hotel, complete with a concierge, restaurant, play area and offers room service and tour guide services. This is not on the beach, though.
NH17; Ph: 08382-266602; www.sterlingholidays.com; Tariff (incl. breakfast, double occupancy): ₹4,500.

GREAT OUTDOORS
Spread over an entire island, this is blessed with great views. It is a good option if you're looking for water sports.
Kurumgad Island; Ph: 0824-4279152, 09844042152; www.thegreatoutdoorsindia.com; Tariff (incl. all meals, double occupancy): ₹3,000.

MAJALI BEACH VILLAGE
Quite elusive, the Majali Beach Village takes a while to find: but the effort is worth it. Spacious, clean rooms keep you happy indoors and the great wild does the same when you step out. Plan an easy-paced holiday here.
Majali Beach Road, Devbagh; Ph: 08382-266891; www.majaliresorts.com; Tariff (incl. breakfast, double occupancy): ₹3,300.

TARANG RESORT
Tarang's location is more of a highlight than the accommodation. It offers large, clean rooms filled with intricately carved furniture, overlooking green lawns. With a restaurant and children's play area, this is a comfortable option for a family holiday.
Maldarwada, Devbagh; Ph: 08382-655850; www.tarangresorts.com; Tariff: ₹2,100.

EATING OUT

There are no good eating options in Karwar. It is recommended that you have your meals at the hotel in which you are staying.

Gorgeous Green

The Brahmagiri Range in Kodagu

Bandipur ▸▸ Kabini ▸▸ Kodagu

VITALS
Getting There
The Bandipur National Park lies over 200km southwest of Bengaluru, and is a good place to start a drive in the greenest slice of Karnataka, along the wildlife belt, melting into the coffee-scaped hills of Kodagu (earlier Coorg). The near-seamless transition from a thick, semi-deciduous forest to the low hills carpeted with coffee is the highlight of the trail. One can start from Bandipur, which is connected by state-run and private buses. Driving through the forest-flanked roads of the Nilgiri Biosphere is the best part of the trip. Spotting elephants, Indian gaur and monkeys is not uncommon.

The closest rail and air junction to Bandipur is Mysuru, the cultural capital of Karnataka. Roads to Bandipur, Kabini and Kodagu radiate from here: Mysuru-south towards Bandipur (77.4km) and Masinagudi in Tamil Nadu (10km further south from Bandipur), southwest to Kabini (59km) and west to Kodagu (117.8km).

Best Time to Go
Kabini and Bandipur can be visited in the months of March to May, if wildlife spotting is on your list. Kodagu is a year-round destination offering multiple months to enjoy its beauty – misty mountains in the winters, March and April for the coffee blooms and as a veritable hill station in the summers. Kodagu also has a number of hikes that make for great summer trips.

> **TOP TIP** Overnight travel to Bandipur is not recommended as the forest road is closed between 6 p.m.–6 a.m. Only one bus goes through the forest gates at night to arrive in Bandipur at about 5 a.m.

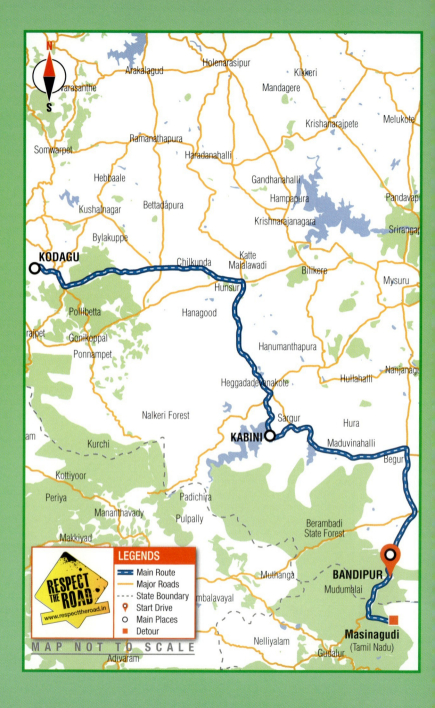

EXPLORING THE CIRCUIT

This chapter takes you into three different regions, all radiating from the central town of Mysuru, making three distinct trips: Kodagu and Bylakuppe, Kabini and Bandipur, and Masinagudi. Rather than coming back to Mysuru every time, one can cut across from Bandipur, straight to Kabini through NH67 and SH86, then further north to Kodagu taking the SH86. While Bandipur, Masinagudi and Kabini are known as wildlife bastions of the state, Kodagu attributes its green draw to the lush coffee estates. These towns make for three different trips for the number of the sights that one can see in each, but given that Mysuru can be kept as base, also make for a good round trip if you have time at hand.

Bandipur is an excellent destination for wildlife enthusiasts as the 880-sqkm (approx.) expanse of the deciduous topography offers more than plenty reasons for a complete wildlife immersion. Sharing its border with other forests like Nagarhole National Park, Mudumalai Sanctuary and the Wayanad Wildlife Sanctuary, this is decidedly one of the best places to see a variety of animals and birds.

Lying at the edge of the Nagarhole forest, Kabini has emerged as one of the best wildlife resort destinations of India, with a

View of Bandipur ▼

Experience Karnataka

number of luxury and mid-range resorts in the vicinity. Many of them overlook the backwaters of the Kabini River that sprawls in front. Jungle safaris, coracle rides, village walks and nature trails are the highlight here. Kabini is the perfect getaway with a blend of luxury and rustic forest life.

Kodagu has earned itself the rightful moniker of the 'adventure capital of Karnataka', with a number of hikes and rafting options from here. On a contrasting note, it is also one of the best places to unwind in the midst of lush coffee plantations. Located on the eastern edge of the Western Ghats, it has the benefit of a diverse topography with mountains, coffee plantations, thick forests and rivers, all making a serene backdrop, ideal to unwind in. These form a suitable backdrop to a number of activities like rafting, kayaking, canoeing, trekking, camping, micro light flying and quad biking.

BANDIPUR

SIGHTSEEING HIGHLIGHTS
Jungle Safari

A wildlife photographer's dream come true, the jungle safari is a major attraction at Bandipur. Elephants, deer and wild boar are fairly easily visible, while deeper in the tufts of bamboo, a stable population of tigers, leopards, gaurs (Indian bison), hyenas and sloth bears can be found. Amongst the birds,

Deer are easily sighted during the jungle safari in Bandipur

Indian silver bill, scaly breasted munia, purple rumped sunbird and the jungle babbler are commonly spotted.

The jeep safaris (45 minutes to 2.5 hours), operated solely by the government enterprise, Jungle Lodges & Resorts (JLR), are the highlight of the destination, with serious wildlife enthusiasts booking as many trips even for a short duration. One is likely to be packed off in a canter-like large truck, so book ahead and ensure that you bag a Gypsy if you can. Since there is a stringent control on the number of vehicles that enter the forest area, be relentlessly timely about this.

Bandipur Forest Information Centre; Ph: 0821-2480902; **Entry Fee**: *Indian: ₹300, Foreigners: ₹1,100;* **Camera**: *₹200;* **Timings**: *6–8 a.m., 3–5 p.m., open all days. Book the safari through your resort for convenience, but they are likely to add an upcharge of ₹250 per head.*

Himavad Gopalaswamy Betta

Drive up for a bird's-eye view of the forest and areas around from the hilltop Krishna temple at 1,455 metres, the highest peak of Bandipur hills. It is a 21-km drive from the Bandipur Check Post. Take left from Mangala village and drive along the bleached rocky terrain.

Timings: *8.30 a.m.–4 p.m., open all days.*

Mangala Village Walk

The Bandipur region has always been the abode for the shepherd Kuruba tribe, who are also adept bee collectors. The Mangala village is home to a set of resorts and some remaining households of the Kurubas. Take a walk in the village with a local for some interaction or just to take a break from the jungle-themed trip.

This activity is included in the package in most resorts.

Birdwatching

Most of the properties in Bandipur are spread over sprawling acres of uncultivated land to maintain a rustic feel. Fortunately, one can spot quite a few species of birds outside the forest area too. Take help from the resident naturalist in your resort.

This activity is included in the package in most resorts.

Experience Karnataka

ACCOMMODATION

BANDIPUR SAFARI LODGE
The JLR (Jungle Lodges & Resorts Ltd.) property offers 22 adequately furnished value-for-money cottages amidst 9.5 acres of land. Look out for artist Sunita Dhiaryam paintings on the walls of five rooms. The Gol Ghar (common gazebo), restaurant and the bonfire area are usually packed with weekend go-oers.

Mysore–Ooty Road, Melukamanahalli, Angala Post, Gundlupet Taluk, Chamrajnagar District; Ph: 08229-233001; www.junglelodges.com; Tariff (full board): ₹6,932–9,493 onwards per day/per head.

DHOLE'S DEN
The eco-conscious luxury homestay on the fringes of the forest has all the trappings of a great stay – rainwater harvesting, wind-turbine-generated electricity (indicated by green switches) and accommodation for only 16 at a time. The rooms at Dhole's Den are dotted with bright animal-themed art and lively furnishings. The food spread is elaborate, yet simple and delicious.

Kaniyinapura Village, Bandipur National Park, Gundlupet Taluk, Chamrajnagar District; Ph: 08229-236062; www.dholesden.com; Tariff (double occupancy, full board): ₹12,000–15,000.

SPECIAL STAYS

Jungle Hut
A combination of luxury tents, an enclosed camping site and deluxe rooms are suitable for large and small groups. The gushing mini-waterfall in the pool area is what keeps guests tethered to the area.

Bokkapuram, Masinagudi, Nilgiri District; Ph: 0423-2526240; www.junglehut.in; Tariff (double occupancy, incl. breakfast, excl. taxes): ₹5,000 onwards.

Jungle Retreat
One of the oldest family-run resorts of the region, Jungle Retreat is one of the best. Owner Rohan Mathias and his well-immersed team ensure that this is suitable for eco-conscious leisure travellers and wildlife enthusiasts. Expect to find it difficult to

THE SERAI BANDIPUR
The property provides a lavish stay in rustic environs. The courtyard, cabin and residence cottages are set amidst 17 acres but have all luxury facilities like spa, pool, indoor games, gym and an extensive restaurant.
Kaniyanapura Village, Chamrajnagar District; Ph: 08229-236075; www.theserai.in; Tariff (double occupancy, full board): ₹14,754 onwards for 3 days, 2 nights.

THE WINDFLOWER TUSKER TRAILS
Tusker Trails offers the perfect blend of forest living and luxury; the newly furbished cottages and suites are camouflaged by a dense copse but include all components of a high-end resort. Here you are unplugged from city life with no TV. The swimming pool overlooking the forest and a massage at Emerge Spa are good additions.
S. No. 125, Mangala Village, Bandipur, Chamrajnagar District; Ph: 08229-236055; www.thewindflower.com; Tariff (double occupancy, full board): ₹23,400 for 3 days, 2 nights.

EATING OUT

Since this is a forest-resort destination, you will not find restaurants in the town. Tourists choose to take packages where food is included.

SHOPPING

Bandipur is no shopping hotspot but souvenirs are well worth your while. Tees, jackets, coasters, magnets and more are available at Temple Tree Designs, the brainchild of Sunita Dhairyam, who has initiated locals' involvement in the shop and the Mariamma Charitable Trust.
The Mariamma Temple Road, Mangala Village, Gundlupet Taluk, Chamrajnagar District; Ph: 09449818796 (Indra Kumar); www.templetreedesigns.com; Timings: 7 a.m.–7 p.m., open all days.

detach yourself from the swimming pool area. The swimming pool is 'chlorine-free' as a number of animals decide to take a swig from it at nights.

Masinagudi, Nilgiri District; Ph: 0423-2526469; www.jungleretreat.com; Tariff: (double occupancy, excl. breakfast & taxes): ₹5,468 onwards.

The Wilds at Northern Hay
This century-old bungalow is in sync with the coffee plantation and forest area around it. The 98-acre expanse of the Wilds at Northern Hay, a private property, allows one to have personalized sighting experiences in the in-house Gypsy. Even when you are at the cottage, you are surrounded by sounds from the jungle.

Singara Post, Masinagudi, Nilgiri District; Ph: 09843149490; www.serendipityo.com; Tariff (double occupancy, incl. breakfast & taxes): ₹6,000 onwards.

DETOUR
Masinagudi

Only 10km south of Bandipur National Park, Masinagudi in the state of Tamil Nadu makes for an unadulterated experience of wildlife with no safaris and tourist clammer. Set in the backdrop of the Mudumalai forest, this is a great place to unwind at a number of eco-inclined resorts and home stays. Even though personal safaris are banned, you are likely to find elephants, bison, gaur, sambhar and deer on a drive on the highway. Leopards frequently visit many properties as well.

The town itself consists of one main street with paltry options for entertainment. One can drive down to Bandipur for the safaris (pg. 148) or go on nature hikes organized by the resort around their properties.

been a habitat for Asian elephants along with other animals like leopards, Indian gaur and wild boar. Safaris can be organized by the resort, provided you book up front.

Entry Fee: Indians (Adult & Child): ₹1,720 & ₹1,520 respectively, Foreigners (Adult & Child): ₹2,720 & ₹2,470, respectively; **Timings**: 5.45–10 a.m., 3–7 p.m., open all days.

Others

Other ways to spend time in the vicinity of the jungle are coracle rides in the backwaters, short nature hikes with naturalists in the outskirts of the jungle and visiting villages that are located close by. This is mostly organized by the resorts, many of which offer cycles for roaming around, and have swimming pools and spas to keep guests entertained.

KABINI

SIGHTSEEING HIGHLIGHTS
Safari in the Nagarhole National Park

The Nagarhole National Park is rife with wildlife, making this a veritable destination for wildlife lovers. Declared a national park in 1974, it has

Elephants strolling along the river at Nagarhole National Park

ACCOMMODATION

THE BISON KABINI WILDLIFE RESORT
A luxury tented set-up on the banks of the backwaters, Bison is the epitome of luxury and complete immersion in wildlife. The owners, Jungs, are the first family of wildlife led by the man of the house, Nawabzada Saad Bin Jung, a well-known novelist and eco-tourism advocate. His son, Shaaz, is a renowned naturalist who you are likely to meet here.
Gundathur Village, Karapura-Kabini Road, Nisana Hobli, HD Kote Taluk; Ph: 08065590271; Tariff (incl. breakfast): ₹2,500.

KABINI LAKE VIEW RESORT
The Jungle Lodges property commands exhilarating views of the backwaters and the jungle. Basic to luxury rooms are available, depending on the budget. This no-frills lodge gives you an option to submerge yourself in all things wildlife than other luxury facilities.
Karapura, Nissana Belthur Post, HD Kote Taluk; Ph: 08228264405; www.junglelodges.com; Tariff (full board): ₹6,960–10,544.

ORANGE COUNTY RESORT
One of the best in the vicinity, Orange County replicates the brand's other models by offering luxury accommodation, though in sync with the wildlife theme. A reading room, Ayurveda-focused spa, swimming pool, Jacuzzi and wildlife-themed activities are the highlights.
Bheeramballi Village & Post, HD Kote Taluk; Ph: 08228-269108; www.orangecounty.in; Tariff (double occupancy packages, incl. all meals, excl. taxes): ₹22,950 onwards.

RED EARTH RESORT
The serene surroundings and the earthy cottages of the resort are the highlight, as is the view of the backwaters from here. Apart from the safaris with experts, the pool is another draw for tourists. Look out for the lean season packages during monsoons.
Badane Kuppe (Near Hosamalla), Via Antharasante, HD Kote Taluk; Ph: 08884733500; www.redearthkabini.in; Tariff (double occupancy, full board, excl. taxes): ₹14,000.

THE SERAI
Though Wildwoods is 85km from Udipi, if you are doing the coastal stretch, this secretive spot is a delight. It sits along a stream and can be reached through a drive between bamboo clusters and forest. The resort lies 6km off the highway but is worth your while for its intimate cottages, well-versed naturalists, excellent Ayurveda facilities and plenty of outdoor activities.
No. 60/1, Nishana, Karapura Village, Antarasante Hobli, HD Kote Taluk; Ph: 08040012200; www.theserai.in; Tariff (double occupancy, full board): ₹13,753 onwards.

WATERWOODS LODGE AND RESORTS
Imagine, your bedroom overlooking a large sprawl of water. Company of great views, excellent food and hospitality is promised at Waterwoods. With the Brahmagiri Range as the backdrop, the lodge is a great choice to unwind.
HD Kote Taluk; Ph: 07022013180; www.wildwoodsspa.com; Tariff (incl. full board & additional activities): ₹5,500–6,500.

EATING OUT

There are no specific restaurants to eat as most resorts offer full board options.

Experience Karnataka

Harangi Dam is a popular camp site (see pg. 157)

KODAGU

SIGHTSEEING HIGHLIGHTS

Raja's Seat
A sunset point, now manicured like a park, Raja's Seat may be touristy but awards one with fantastic views of the valley below. It also serves as a seasonal garden with fountains. Weary tourists are often seen here sitting and relaxing after a day of sightseeing.

Entry Fee: ₹5; *Timings*: Sunrise to Sunset.

Dubare Elephant Camp
Watch the bathing and feeding of elephants at the edge of the Cauvery River at the Dubare Elephant Camp. These elephants are retired from the forest department. The camp also organizes coracle rides. This is an all-year-round activity, but the best season to go here is between September to March.

Charges: Boating: ₹20, Rafting: ₹1,000, Bathing elephants: ₹100, Elephant ride (not recommended): ₹100; *Timings*: 10 a.m.–5 p.m., the bathing only at 10 a.m.

Iruppu Falls
Located at the base of the Brahmagiri Trek, the falls are a popular hotspot on weekends. Also known as the Lakshmana Tirtha Falls, this is the place where the tributary of Cauvery, Lakshmana Tirtha River, originates. A famous Shiva temple, the Rameshwara Temple, marks the place.

Timings: Sunrise to Sunset.

Tala Kaveri

The source of the River Cauvery, commemorated by a small temple at the base of the Brahmagiri Hill, is known as Tala Kaveri. The temple here is dedicated to Goddess Kaveriamma and sees a number of pilgrims who come to visit annually.

Timings: *Sunrise to Sunset.*

Omkareshwara Temple

This temple is dedicated to Shiva, and was built in 1820 by Lingarajendra II. Constructed in the Muhammadan-style of architecture, it has a dome at the centre and four turrets at four corners. The Omkareshwara Temple is one of the key highlights of Madikeri. A visit here is a must on the sightseeing trail of Kodagu.

Timings: *Sunrise to Sunset.*

Nisargadhama

A 'picnicky' vibe to the Nisargadhama Island off Kushalnagar makes it hardly the pick for tourists with discretion, but it is something to check off the list in Kodagu. A hanging rope bridge is the highlight of the place. It is also a base for rafting in the Cauvery River, which flows down till the Dubare Elephant Camp.

Timings: *9 a.m.–5 p.m.*

BYLAKUPPE

One of the largest Tibetan settlements in India, Bylakuppe is situated 40km away from Kodagu, before Kushalnagar, when travelling from Mysuru. Lugsum Samdupling in 1961 and Dickyi Larsoe in 1969 established it. Reserve a few hours for Bylakuppe, turning left 6km before Kushalnagar to see the Namdroling Monastery and the Golden Temple that stand in commemoration to Buddhist gurus.

Also see the Serpom Monastic University, Sakya Monastery, Sera Mey Monastery and University. A Buddhist settlement in the heart of Karnataka is testament to the diverse social fabric of the state.

Abbey Falls

The sylvan setting of the gushing water and the lush coffee states around is reason enough to visit Abbey Falls. It looks especially robust just after the monsoons. The place is over-treaded so picking an off-season to visit may be ideal.

Entry Fee: *₹5;* **Timings**: *9 a.m.–5 p.m.*

Experience Karnataka

KODAGU AS AN ADVENTURE DESTINATION

Rafting
Rafting in the Upper Barapole (Kithu-Kakkatu River) to manoeuvre Grade 1–4 rapids with Coorg White Water Rafting is a great addition to your trip. Encounter rapids like Morning Coffee (level 1), Grasshopper (level 2), Ramba Samba (level 2), Wicked Witch (level 3) and the Big Band (level 4).

Ponya Estate (Off T. Shettigeri); Ph: 09481883745; www.coorgwhitewaterrafting.com;
Rates: ₹1,200 per head (3-4 hours, including jeep pick-up, gear, tea, use of the base camp); Photographs with own camera are free, additional ₹100 for professional photographs and video; Time slots: 9 a.m., 11 a.m., 2 p.m. & 4 p.m.

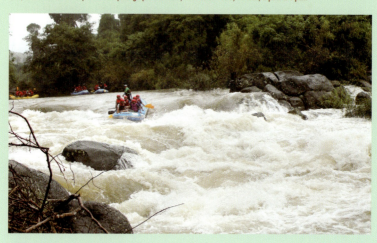

Micro Light Flying (Off Kutta/Gonikoppa)
Coorg Sky Adventures run by Muthanna offers the chance to fly in 2-seater open craft at a maximum height of 3,500 feet above the ground. The sport is sensitive to weather and dependent on the time of the day, so one must stay in touch with Muthanna before arriving here, in case there are any changes. The most suitable weather is between November and May. There is a weight limit of upto 90kg and children above 7 years are allowed. Use your discretion if you are a heart patient or have any altitude-related disorder. There's no doubt that photographers interested in aerial photography will love this.

Ponnampet (Off Gonikoppa); Ph: 09448954384; www.coorgskyadventures.com;
Rates: 10 minutes/₹2,250 per head, 30 minutes (50km)/₹5,000 per head, 60 minutes (100km)/₹8,000 per head.

Kayaking & Canoeing (Off Kakkabe)
Enjoy the low-key parts of the Cauvery River with Jungle Mount Adventures at their 7-acre campsite, wedged between a paddy field and the Cauvery River. The 20-feet

deep stretch of the river at the edge of the camp is perfect to enjoy the 3-man kayaks and 2-man canoes with instructors.

Kakkabe Village, Yavakapady Post; Ph: 09845831675; www.junglemountadventures.com;
Tariff (incl. full board & activities): ₹3,200 per head.

Quad Biking & More (Off Kakkabe)
Indo-British company Now or Neverland is a good addition in your holiday itinerary in Kodagu if you want to try your hand at quad biking, the jungle gym, paint ball and mountain biking. It is off road, through the forests and slushy tracks on a 1-km circuit on an instructor-led loop. Also try your hand at an obstacle course sprinkled with walkways, bridges and tunnels with ropes, zip lines and strong wires.

Ph: 08274-323023; www.noworneverland.com

Camping & Kayaking by the Harangi Waters (Off Kushal Nagar)
Camp in the backwaters of the Harangi Dam, just off Kushalnagar. Eco Habitat (14km from this spot) facilitates this at the 3-acre personal camping spot. Though day trips can also be organized, ensure that you take in the whole experience by starting in the afternoon from Eco Habitat, indulging in water sports and then camping by the water. There is a small utility area with a basic toilet close to the camping spot. Packed food, a barbecue and wood for a bonfire can be made available for an additional cost.

Ph: 09448127245; www.ecohabitat.in; Camping Site at Narkur Village;
Rates: ₹500 per tent, sleeping mats and air pillows (a deposit of ₹2,500 is refundable. Carry your own sleeping bag); ₹1,500 for group of 4 for barbecue set-up, ₹100–300 for full-night fire; ₹500 for watchman if you require; ₹100 for BSNL phone for hire in case you want to get in touch; Kayaking/Canoeing: ₹250 per head (max. 200kg, children above 5 years allowed).

Hikes/Treks
- Drive on the Madikeri–Mangaluru Road, 10km off the Toll Junction to touch a small village called Manangeri. Enjoy an exhilarating 4-wheel drive for about 5km up the hill on the right, and then hike up to the Manangeri Ridge. The hike is only about 2km, and is easy for children as well. Hire a jeep from Madikeri (₹1,000 one way). Ask the driver to wait for a couple of hours so you can return in the same jeep.
- The forested Brahmagiri Range overlooks southern parts of Kodagu. The challenging Brahmagiri Trek (off Kutta) is moderate to difficult, with excellent opportunity to spot wild animals and be in the core region of Kodagu's impressive bio diversity.
- The highest peak of Kodagu is a short but demanding stretch of 5km. Tadiandamol Trek (off Kakkabe) is one of the most popular treks with people graduating from beginners to amateurs. The peak rewards one with excellent views of stacked mountains and dipping valleys between them.

Experience Karnataka

HOCKEY

Few people might know, but Kodagu has a long association with the game of field hockey. More than fifty Kodavas (local Coorgis) have represented India in international hockey tournaments, of which seven have also participated in the Olympics. Every year, the Kodava Hockey Festival is held in different parts of the district in April, where families participate in the very competitive tournament.

ACCOMMODATION

BEL HOME
The 1928-built cottages are ideal to relax in the coffee plantation after crossing the Madapura River. This also has great access to Kotta Betta (third highest peak of Kodagu). Bel Home provides an ideal stay for those who want to learn about coffee; third-generation planters, Vijay and his wife Ramola are excellent company and take great interest in your comfort, ensuring that you get a taste of the real Kodagu with a 'bean to cup' coffee experience, local food, birdwatching and places to see.
Bellarimotte Estate, Madapura Post; Ph: 09880908135; www.bellhome.co.in; Tariff (incl. full board): ₹4,200.

BISON MANOR
Opt for Bison Manor if you're for company of the namesake animals. Run by Hugh and Vivian, this has the vibe of an old Coorgi home but fitted with all modern amenities. Pick the first-floor rooms for a view of the Brahmagiri Range from your sit-out.
New Grand Estate, Kutta; Ph: 08105118877; www.bisonmanor.com; Tariff (incl. full board): ₹3,900.

CHINGAARA
A nature-inclined resort on a 12-acre plantation, which shares the boundary with Honey Valley, one needs to get here by a 4-wheel jeep. A massive private waterfall welcomes you as soon as you enter Chingaara. Enjoy the company of a number of dogs and Lily the donkey while you stay here.
Yavakapady Village Post, Kabinakkad; Ph: 08272-204488; www.chingaara.com; Tariff (incl. full board): ₹1,800/2,300/2,500 onwards.

ECO HABITAT
Exclusive cottages with personal splash pools attached to the villa is the highlight of this stay. Add to that, perfect hosts in Som and Chethana, and the trip only has to be memorable. If not the stay, visit Eco Habitat for Chethana's delicious lemon grass tea and each meal better than the previous one. Meet other tourists in the common pavilion that is used as a dining space. Privacy, great company of hosts and an informative stay in Kodagu are the reasons why one should pick Eco Habitat.
Chikbettagere Village, Guddehosur Post, Kushalnagar; Ph: 09448127245; www.ecohabitat.in; Tariff (incl. full board): ₹5,000, lunch and dinner at ₹250 per meal/per head.

GOWRI NIWAS
Despite being situated in the heart of Madikeri town, Gowri Niwas seems like a secret with an exclusive stay option with only three cottages and a small garden in front. An earthy feel with classy wooden furniture and charming bric-a-bracs makes the stay charming
P.O. Box 138, New Ext Madikeri; Ph: 08272-228597; www.gowrinivas.com; Tariff (incl. breakfast): ₹3,800.

HONEY VALLEY

Add to your adventure experience by staying at the remote Honey Valley resort, tucked away like a secret on a 30-acre coffee plantation and which can be reached by a 4-wheel vehicle. The resort is good for serious nature lovers. The main reason why one should opt for this is the exclusive trek to Tadiandamol, which is much longer (18km/7 hours) and consists of largely cattle tracks. Book ahead and discuss your stay with Mr Chengappa before arriving.

P.O. Yavakapady; Ph: 08272-238339; www.honeyvalleyindia.in; Tariff: (incl. full board):₹450 onwards without attached loos, Eastside Doubles: ₹400–990, Perch Doubles: ₹1,150–2,000, Tranquil Doubles: ₹1,300–1,800; Additional ₹400 for all meals; Additional cost: for Guide: ₹400, for Transport: ₹150, for Camp Fire: ₹400.

MISTY WOODS

Suitable for families, Misty Woods offers comfortable cottages play areas and a small waterfall. Though the old-styled roofs have been emulated for aesthetics, the look and feel of the resort is modern.

Near Nalknad Palace, Kakkabe; Ph: 08272-238561; www.coorgmisty.com; Tariff: (incl. full board): ₹7,500 onwards.

PALACE ESTATE

The bright, wooden double-storeyed structure of Palace Estate with a manicured garden all around is a pleasant break from the shaded coffee plantation stays of Kodagu. If you have an option, ask for the first-floor rooms as they have a better view. This is the closest homestay to Tadiandamol.

Kakkabe, Near Nalknad Palace; Ph: 08272-238446; www.palaceestate.co.in; Tariff: ₹3,100/3,600 onwards.

SILVER BROOK ESTATE

A hand-picked collection of wooden furniture and the small library unit are the best part of Silver Brooks Estate. The rooms too are well furnished and spacious. The stone pillar bases are designed as board games, which is a hit with children.

Kadagadal Village; Ph: 08272-200107; www.silverbrookestate.com; Tariff (incl. breakfast, Executive/Superior Executive/Special Executive Rooms): ₹3,300/3,600/4,250.

TAMARA

Rough it out on the slopes of Tadiandamol and then relax in the super-luxurious wooden cottages with a private deck overlooking rows of coffee bushes of the 174-acre plantation. The in-house coffee shop, The Verandah, follows a coffee theme and is as informative as it is aesthetically charming. The no-children policy at Tamara may appeal to tourists who would like to have some peace.

Kabinakkad Estate, Napoklu Nad, Yavakapadi Village; Ph: 08884000040; www.thetamara.com; Tariff (double occupancy, incl. all meals, excl. taxes): ₹18,000/25,000.

VICTORIAN VERANDAZ

Perfect for a family, the two rooms and a dining area are a great staying option. The view of the valley below, a jeep drive through the thick coffee plantation and delicious food are the highlights of Victorian Verandaz. The homestay is just off Madikeri; central to reach other parts of Kodagu for adventure activities.

Modur Estate, Kadagadal Post; Ph: 09448059850; www.livingcoorg.com; Tariff (incl. breakfast): ₹2,500.

EATING OUT

There are a number of restaurants in Madikeri, but one that food lovers should not miss is the old establishment, Kodagu cuisine. Try the Ghee Rice and Pandi Curry (pork curry). The unassuming place is one of the most celebrated places for the local Kodagu cuisine.

Stuart Hill, Madikeri; Timings: 11 a.m.-8 p.m.; Meal for 2: ₹500.

Coffee & Treks

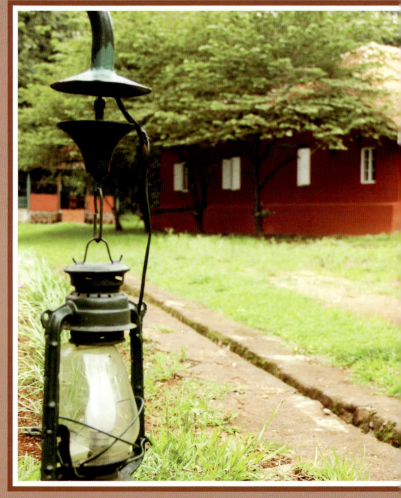

Hunkal Woods is one of the staying options in Chikmagalur

Hassan ▶▶ Chikmagalur

VITALS
Getting There
Hassan lies 185km from Bengaluru on NH48. An excellent highway ensures that one takes not more than 3 hours to get to the base for tracing the Hoysala history in nearby Belur (approx. 40km from Hassan) and Halebeedu (approx. 32km from Hassan). The SH57, a smooth road with a few ghat sections, joins Hassan and Chikmagalur (also known as Chikmagaluru). While the Hassan–Belur–Halebeedu is a sector that can be traversed separately, especially by history enthusiasts (pg. 98), Hassan to Chikmagalur and around is a trail filled with a million shades of green. The coffee-scaped undulating hills, fractured by the Bhadra River and home to the highest peak of the state, this circuit promises a cathartic trip for coffee lovers. One can also do the trail the other way round. Chikmagalur lies at a drivable distance of 245km from Bengaluru and is one of the most travelled routes on NH75 on weekends. It takes about 5 hours with stops.

Best Time to Go
Chikmagalur is a great all-year-round destination, though when the coffee blooms announce a good bounty in the month of March, watching the green hills change to a carpet of white is fascinating. Some might say that the monsoons can be ruthless, but those of you who like the sound of rain and wear adventure on their sleeve, you can explore rafting down the Bhadra.

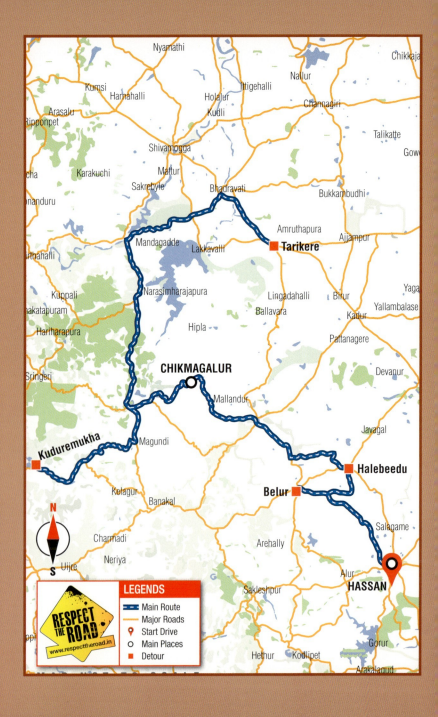

EXPLORING THE CIRCUIT

The birthplace of coffee cultivation in India and now a major hub that is the source base for one of the most popular coffee brands in India, Chikmagalur is where it all started. India owes its coffee lineage to Sufi pilgrim, Baba Budangiri, who managed to smuggle in seven beans from his trip to Mecca in the seventeenth century, and plant it in the perfect altitude of Chikmagalur. Here the plants flourished and created an economy that has stayed with generations ahead. Till date, the Kathlekhan Estate, now owned by the largest producers of coffee in India, Café Coffee Day group, bears testimony to this great bit of history.

Chikmagalur has evolved into one of the largest production hubs of coffee in India and is also one of the homestay bastions of the country. Given its ideal environs, many coffee planters opened their homes and plantations to guests to have a relaxing time. Ecologically inclined, many owners strive hard to not over commercialize the destination and keep its natural resources in check.

The perfect active getaway is sprinkled with heritage spots and adventure options in close vicinity of wildlife and nature. Home to the highest mountain range of Karnataka, Mullayangiri, Chikmagalur is a popular trekking option from Bengaluru. You can choose between the big mountain loop of Mullayangiri, Baba Budangiri Hill and Kemmanagundi or the Kudremukh, Horanadu and Bhadra River sector.

AN ALL-YEAR-ALL-ROUND DESTINATION

From whichever angle you look at Chikmagalur, it is suitable for all age-groups and for people of all tastes and preferences – as a kid-friendly destination, as one for rafting enthusiasts, or for birders, for beginner and skilled trekkers, for those seeking spiritual bliss or for those who might have decided to do nothing on their trip. A destination that is excellent at any time of the year and offers a range of things to do, Chikmagalur is possibly one of the most enthralling parts of Karnataka. Add to that, it encompasses a large region, making driving in the hills an absolute pleasure.

SIGHTSEEING HIGHLIGHTS
Chikmagalur's Mountain Loop

The most talked about spots in Chikmagalur lie on this loop that makes for a great drive and takes an entire day. Go past the city towards Kaimara to start at the foothills and head straight towards Sheethalagiri, a 1,000-year-old Mallikarjuna Temple. The shrine itself is an

Experience Karnataka

The Mallikarjunaswamy Temple, dedicated to Lord Shiva, is a historic temple

unassuming one, but is worth your while for its age and the *prasadam*, (an offering of food that is offered to the deity and thereafter distributed amongst devotees) a fistful of water from a natural pool inside (**Timings**: sunrise to sunset). Next on the circuit is the Baba Budangiri Hill, also known as the Dattagiri Hill Range (Inam Dattatreya Peetha), after the famous saint. This small shrine is perched at 1,895 metres and affords breathtaking views from the top – there is something more spiritual than the religious hook of this place. The shrine is visited by both Hindus and Muslims. The next stop is Mullayangiri, the highest peak (1,930 metres) in the state. Expectedly windy and cold, even in summers, it's suitable to stay for a short time to enjoy the misty views of the valley below. The peak is covered in Kurinji flowers when it blooms in periods of 12 years. The next blooms are slated for 2020.

Kemmanagundi

After having experienced the higher peaks of Mullayangiri and Baba Budangiri Hills, a trip to Kemmanagundi seems rather plain, but it makes for an ideal low-intensity trip. A small, unimpressive rock garden and a government-run children's park is avoidable. Apart from the view of the coffee-clad hills from here, the only reason why one

> ## TREKKING TO MULLAYANGIRI
>
> Nirvana Nomads organizes treks and adventure trips all over the country, but are veritable experts of the state. Join them for the Mullayangiri Trek for a hassle-free time. The fun company and knowledge of the place are their strong points. (Ph: 09916596159; www.nirvananomads.com; Cost: Trekking with rafting: ₹4,950 per head, Only trekking: ₹3,950 per head, ex-Bengaluru, incl. travel, food, stay, instructors.)
>
> India Hikes organizes treks in the country. Even though the Mullayangiri Trek can be done on your own, they can assist you with a guide, camping and permissions. (Ph: 09590363344; www.indiahikes.com; Brundavana, 1st Floor, Plot No. 36, 1st Main Road, Dena Bank Colony, Ganga Nagar, Bengaluru.)

should visit this place, is because it is the access point for the stunning Hebbe Falls.

Hebbe Falls

From Kemmanagundi, Hebbe Falls is a thrilling off-road drive of 13km, which can only be done in a 4-wheel vehicle. Rusted and rickety, but oddly sturdy, 'Commander' jeeps are available on hire (₹400 per head in a shared vehicle) for a round trip. The last stretch to the falls has to be traversed on foot, hopping over shallow rocky stream at two points. The effort is worth your while as

▲ Hebbe Falls is one of the most picturesque tourist destinations

Experience Karnataka

> **TOP TIP**: Carry a small packet of salt with you to release pesky leeches from your feet. These are usually found in the monsoons, but Hebbe Falls lie in a dense, shaded forest, making the environment moist and conducive for them at all times.

you watch a cascade of frothy white fall from a craggy cliff top – a 55-feet drop from top.

*Near Kemmangundi, Chikmagalur; **Entry Fee**: ₹10; **Car parking**: ₹50; **Timings**: 8 a.m.–5 p.m.; open all days.*

Coffee beans aplenty

Kalhatti Falls

From Kemmanagundi, the drive to Kalhatti is only 10km. It is more of a religious stop with a Lord Veerabhadra Temple in the middle of the stream. The Kalhatti Falls pale compared to the glorious Hebbe Falls where the mammoth cascade of water trumps with the sheer magnitude of water.

Coffee Yatra

An initiative of the Coffee Board of India, the Coffee Yatra is a thematic display of coffee history, processes and types in the region. The Coffee Museum also has a lab where one can see the demonstration for grinding and other paraphernalia used in coffee processing. Unfortunately, a tasting experience is missing – that would have completed the picture for the tourist.

*Coffee Centre, Behind ZP Office, Kadur Road, Chikmagalur; **Entry Fee**: Adults & Children: ₹20; **Timings**: 10 a.m.–1 p.m., 2–5.30 p.m., open all days except weekends and general holidays.*

Horanadu

Horanadu is an important pilgrimage centre in Chikmagalur and is known for the idol of Annapurneshwari, which was installed by Adi Shankaracharya. Queue up in a long but fast-moving line to get a quick glimpse of the goddess and be ushered out with velocity by strict priests. If you are not religiously inclined, go there for the simple but tasteful food served as *prasadam* every day. Thousands sit in neat rows on the floor while priests serve Malnad-style food in an efficient manner.

Horanadu Temple, Chikmagalur;
Timings: *lunch: Noon–2.30 p.m., dinner: 8–9.45 p.m., open all days.*

Belavadi

A pleasant break from the overly touristy places in Chikmagalur or the Hoysala sector, the Belavadi Temple is ideal for those who have a taste for the offbeat. Part of the Hoysala trail, but off the main circuit, Belavadi falls 29km from Chikmagalur. More than a hundred soap stone pillars meet you in the main hall. Three shrines of Lord Vishnu – Narayana, Venugopala and Yoganarsimha – lie on three sides of the temple. The temple is also mentioned in the Mahabharata as the location where the demon, Bakasura, was slain.

WHITE-WATER RAFTING IN BHADRA

Choose a day of rafting to add a dimension of adventure to your Chikmagalur trip. The frothy and bubbling Bhadra River that runs for 10km in the Kudremukh National Park is a perfect river to fine-tune your skills on the rapids or just enjoy bouncing over them with experts, with abandon. The best person to help you plan a day-long adventure on the river is Krishna from Capture, an outdoor outfit operating in the region for a long time. (Ph: 09845355087; www.capture-earth.com; call for different packages ranging from a few hours to the whole day.)

Belavadi Temple, Chikmagalur;
Timings: *Sunrise to Sunset.*

The Belavadi Temple, dedicated to Lord Vishnu

ACCOMMODATION

BALUR ESTATE
How about 400 acres of coffee plantation and a ludicrous amount of green for company? That and more is promised at the very earthy Balur Estate. A refurbished planter's house from the 1800s ensures that the vibe is still intact. Immerse in the fascinating history of the Indian coffee heritage, while you hear the sound of River Hemavathy in the vicinity — the river originates just above the estate. Urging you to 'do nothing', this one just pushes the need for lazy holidays a notch higher.
Balur Estate, Chikmagalur; Ph: 09590050001; www.linger-at-balur.in;
Tariff (incl. all meals & taxes): ₹2,750.

COFFEE VILLAGE RETREAT
There are two choices for accommodation at Coffee Village Retreat — a 150-year-old colonial plantation bungalow and a contemporary luxury unit. A unique set-up between a 300-acre coffee estate provides proximity to the estate functioning. You can also choose from activities like indoor games, cycling, birdwatching, trekking, boating, fishing or just relaxing by the bonfire.
Kimmane Plantation, Billur Post, Mudigere, Chikmagalur; Ph: 08262229599;
www.coffeevillageretreat.com; Tariff (double occupancy bungalow/luxury unit, incl. all meals & taxes): ₹5,000/7,000.

FLAMEBACK LODGES
Choose from villas, suites and cottages at Flameback. The highlights of the property include wooden sunning decks, personal Jacuzzis and a pool, apart from its stunning location. A break from the coffee topography alone, the lodge also has views of a lake, waterfall and paddy fields. The fact that there are only 8 rooms available ensures an intimate holiday with friends and family. There are three dogs on the property, in case you're fond of them.
Karthikeya Coffee Plantation, Billur Post, Pattadur, Chikmagalur, Mudigere; Ph: 08263-215170; www.flameback.in; Tariff (double occupancy, incl. all meals, spa & on-site activities): ₹12,000–17,500.

HUNKAL WOODS
Hunkal Woods is a great fit for both family getaways and adventure groups with its options of comfortable cottages and camp-like setting. Veterans in coffee plantations, this is a great place to get oriented to the plantation life. Hunkal Woods offers interesting trails like a graveyard walk, sambhar track and those apt for birdwatching. Flanked by the forest and coffee plantations, wildlife spotting is easy from here. The fact that there is a special rate for elders and that it is a pet-friendly property makes it a great option.
Thogarihunkal Group Estates, Chikmagalur; Ph: 09886000788; www.hunkalwoods.com; Tariff (double occupancy): ₹5,000.

THE SERAI
For a plush holiday, choose The Serai (a holding of Coffee Day). Well-organized visits to the plantations, learning about processes as well as coffee tasting (only for checked-in guests) is available. Luxury stay was first introduced by The Serai, with Oma Spa, personal pool or Jacuzzi with every villa.
KM Road, Mugthihalli Post, Chikmagalur; Ph: 08262-224903; www.theserai.in; Tariff (double occupancy): ₹7,462 onwards.

THOTADHAHALLI
Stay here to be in close proximity to the Mullayangiri circuit. Highlights include authentic Malnad food and aesthetically charming rooms. It's a great choice for families where kids can stay on the mezzanine floor of the room. A sprawl of bonsai plants and painstakingly collected antiques dot the house.
Thotadhahalli Estate, Kaimara Post; Ph: 08262-320655; www.thotadahalli.com; Tariff: (double occupancy, incl. all meals & taxes): ₹6,000.

VILLA URVINKHAN
The luxury homestay with 5 cottages is tucked away in the middle of a 400-acre estate, which has been here since the 1800s. Shwetha and Sunil's effort to provide a luxurious stay in the middle of a rugged coffee plantation is amped up by an infinity pool, marvellous aesthetics, fireplaces, restored antique furniture and a delicious spread of local and Continental food.
Niduvale, Mudigere, Chikmagalur; Ph: 09449651400; www.villaurvinkhan.com; Tariff (double occupancy): ₹10,000.

WOODWAYS
Pioneering the homestays scene in the region, Sushmita and Shreedev have run Woodways for over a decade. Expect great company, personally led plantation walks with Shreedev and delicious home-made food. Staying with the couple is a great orientation to Chikmagalur, who are passionate about their hometown and are deeply involved in conservation activities. The home is tastefully furnished and comfortable. Ask for a room with the fireplace for a snug hill-station feeling.
Jakkanhalli Post, Chikmagalur; Ph: 09663071775; www.woodwayhomestay.com; Tariff (double occupancy, incl. all meals, plantation walk, bonfire, taxes): ₹7,000; the owners prefer if you stay for 2 days at least.

EATING OUT
Most tourists like to eat at the homestays and resorts themselves, as the coffee estates are far from each other. However, if you're in town, try the restaurants, given below.

FOOD PALACE
This is a good stop for a snack of south Indian food or slightly more elaborate Indianized Chinese. Nothing worth writing home about, though the service is efficient for the amount of people milling here.
RG Road, Chikmagalur; Ph: 08262-228116; Timings: 7 a.m.–9.30 p.m.; Meal for 2: ₹250–500.

TOWN CANTEEN
For a bite of south Indian food, go to the oldest joint in the city! The restaurant is 52 years old, and a veritable landmark for old timers. The unassuming wooden benches and small set-up tell tales from a bygone era.
RG Road, Chikmagalur; Ph: 08262-222325; Timings: Sun–Fri: 11.30 a.m.–2.30p.m, 6.30–8.30 p.m.; Sat: 1–8.30 p.m.; Meal for 2: ₹250–500.

SHOPPING FOR COFFEE

HUNKAL HEIGHTS
Watch the different processes of coffee making – including the grinding process – and pick up a pack of fresh authentic Chikmagalur Coffee from Hunkal Woods. Add a stay to this, at their homestay and each time you sip their coffee, you will be transported to Chikmagalur's dense coffee plantations.
KM Road, Chikmagalur; Ph: 08262-230472; Timings: 10 a.m.–5.30 p.m.

PANDURANGA COFFEE WORKS
Though coffee is best consumed fresh, if you must carry a souvenir back, try the well-known Panduranga shop on MG Road. It is a one-stop shop for locally branded coffee.
PB No. 150, MG Road, Chikmagalur; Ph: 08262-235345; Timings: 9 a.m.–9.30 p.m.

Kudremukh, from a distance

DETOUR
Kudremukh

The horse-shaped mountain (literal translation of Kudremukh from Kannada) lies in the southwest corner of Chikmagalur. Trekking to the peak is a fun but challenging experience and is not recommended for kids or elderly travellers. The topography ranges from lush Shola forests, brimming with wildlife to sun-bleached grasslands before you hit the summit. Expect to spot deer, wild boars, sambhars and, if you are lucky, even a herd of bison. The trek is about 9.5km long (one way) and takes a good 8-9 hours to complete. There is one main popular route, which is supported by local guides and travel infrastructure, especially one elderly guide by the name of Rajappa.

The Kudremukh trekking trail lies inside the Kudremukh National Park; one needs permission from the Office of the Range Forest Officer (Ph: 09480807653, **Timings**: 10.30 a.m.–5.30 p.m.; **Trek Fee**: ₹75; **Forest Entry Fee**: ₹200; **Guide Fee**: ₹500) in the town, to enter the park. Most trekkers omit this step by engaging Rajappa (Ph: 09481179008/08263-249333) to arrange everything in advance.

Hoysala Trail

The Hoysala Empire (11th–14th century) left their imprint of brilliant architectural splendour on Karnataka in the form of the Halebeedu, Belur, Somanathapura and many other temples. It's best to base yourself in Hassan (pg. 99) to explore these, but if you're in the region for longer, this is easily doable from Chikmagalur.

River Tern Lodge

Situated at the edge of the backwaters of the Bhadra dam, the River Tern Lodge offers a blend of adventure and nature, with a plush option to stay. Given that this is a part-government venture of Jungle Lodges & Retreat (JLR), the proximity to the Bhadra Tiger Reserve (4km) and the vantage location at the edge of the backwaters makes this a gorgeous location. The highlight of the lodge is the view of thousands of river tern birds that congregate at an island during the breeding season in the summers on the semi-submerged islands in the reservoir. Expert-led water activities like kayaking, birdwatching, short hikes and fishing are popular with the guests, making the place highly recommended for families and group outings. Expect to be engaged through the day, followed by relaxed evenings near the bonfire area and delicious meals at the Gol Ghar (common dining pavilion).

River Tern Lodge lies 92km (2 hours) north of Chikmagalur.

JLR properties gently blend in with its surroundings

Behind Ranganathaswamy Temple, Bhadra Project, Lakkavalli; Ph: 08261-215425; www.junglelodges.com; Tariff (double occupancy, incl. all meals, excl. taxes & forest entry fee): ₹6,000.

Sylvan Track

Handicrafts in a Kadumane shop

Shimoga ▸▸ Hubli/Dharwad ▸▸ Dandeli

VITALS
Getting There
Running almost parallel to the west coast of Karnataka is another trail from Shimoga (Shivamoga) to Dandeli, through Hubli and Dharwad, but before that it offers a chance to detour into Davangere and Chitradurga. Shimoga is well connected by train and overnight state-run and private buses. Hubli has an airport with limited connectivity, but ample for tourists who want to explore this route – like Dandeli is often plugged with Jog Falls (pg. 131), if exploring only the northwest part of the state, but makes perfect sense to end this trip on a lush green note.

It's best to drive through the towns to explore and stopping as you please, as local buses take longer routes and stop frequently, consuming a few more hours than the car. Hiring a cab for a day will cost ₹1,500–2,000, depending on the car. The trail, with detours, is not more than 450km, but is best broken into several days.

Best Time to Go
The cooler months from October to February are ideal for this circuit. Dandeli alone is better just after the monsoons when it's rife with a million shades of green.

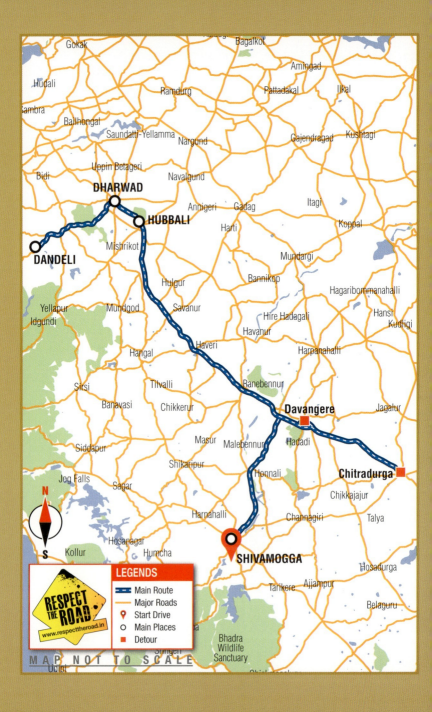

EXPLORING THE CIRCUIT

Suffused in greenery and history, this trail offers unexpected and largely untreaded gems, be it the stunning rustic countryside or the ancient temples that are not pegged on the popular travel sectors. Shimoga is mostly known as the gateway to the Malenadu region of the state, with history steeped in remnants of the Keladi Nayaka rule. Move northeast, towards Davangere, and you're met with delicious cuisine – a blend of north and south Karnataka – especially with the famous Benne Dosa made of rice flour. If nothing else, this dosa definitely deserves a stop. Another worthy reason is the Guladiki Unndi, a special sweet only made in the city.

Chitradurga also makes for a great detour for half a day. The imprint of the Chalukyas, Hoysalas and the Vijayanagar kings still lies on the fort here, making it an incredible destination for history enthusiasts.

Moving north, Hubli, the second-largest city in the state after Bengaluru, is an important hub and known for a few key sightseeing spots like the Unkal Lake and Nrupatunga Hill. A prosperous city, it's got decent infrastructure to spend a day and then move towards Dandeli. Dharwad, on the outskirts, deserves a short stop to sample the Dharwad Petha. Finally, Dandeli is a go-to destination for rafting in the Kali River and being immersed in nature's bounty with many interesting sightseeing spots. Reserve more days for this.

The greenery in Karnataka is a rejuvenating sight

SHIMOGA

Abundant with breathtaking natural beauty, Shimoga is a low-key destination with superlative experiences in store. Fringed by the Sharavathi Valley on the west, there is no dearth of green around here. The adjoining areas like Jog Falls (pg. 131) and Dandeli give it a vibrant stroke of nature's best, and then there is ample history in the Keladi temples (pg. 133), which lies close. In fact, many times, Jog Falls and places around are combined with this. When planning a trip, see if you can combine Jog Falls and the places around.

SIGHTSEEING HIGHLIGHTS

Sakrebailu Elephant Camp

Located 14km from Shimoga, the Sakrebailu Elephant Camp lies on the Thirthahalli Rood. The camp houses a number of elephants that can be seen bathing or being fed by mahouts between 8.30–11 a.m.

Entry Fee: Indians: ₹100, Foreigners: ₹300.

Kodachadri Peak

Try your hand, rather sinew, at the tenth highest peak of Karnataka, towering over the Mookambika Temple in Kollur at 1,343 metres. The name of the hill is derived from the words 'Kodacha' and 'Adri', which in the local language mean, 'home of the jasmine flowers'. When climbing the peak, you are in the middle of the Mookambika National Park. The state has also declared this as a spot of National Heritage. Expect to cross a number of small rivulets, a carpet of bleached grasslands and thickets.

Honnemaradu

A hamlet at the edge of the reservoirs of the Sharavathi River,

▼ An elephant relaxes as the sun sets on the Sakrebailu Elephant Camp

Honnemaradu is one of the lesser-known places off Shimoga. The sprawling backwaters can be traversed in local boats and coracles. The watery expanse is also used for some water-based adventure activities but this is not regular on the calendar.

DETOUR
Davangere
Davangere lies 92km northeast of Shimoga. This small town is famous for its unique cuisine, which has shaped from influences from the northern and southern parts of the state. Benne Dosa is the key highlight here. It is essentially a butter dosa, but originates from here and is loved all over Karnataka.

Chitradurga
Chitradurga lies 60km southeast of Davangere. Chitradurga Fort goes back in time to the Mahabharata. Later, the fort was under Timmana Nayaka, a military serviceman of the Vijayanagar Empire in the sixteenth century. The Nayaka family occupied the fort for over a century, before it fell in the hands of Hyder Ali. The topography of the region is dramatic, especially if one is standing on top of the fort hill. Apart from the fort, one can visit the ancient Chandravalli Caves.

Entry Fee: Indians: ₹5, Foreigners: ₹100;
Timings: 6 a.m.–6 p.m.

JYOTHI RAJ
The rocky terrain of the Chitradurga Fort and surrounding areas, lends itself to rock climbing. A number of experts use the area to whet their skills, but there is one person who visitors specifically look out for – Jyothi Raj (also known as Kothi Raju or Monkey King). A climbing wonder, he is often seen showing off his prowess near the first few gates of the fort. Jyothi Raj is a national climbing champion, who is famous for scaling the heights without any gear or accessories. Given his tryst with climbing, monikers like 'monkey man' and 'spider man' are often associated with him.

ACCOMMODATION

ASHOKA GRAND
The hotel offers budget facilities that are ample for a night's stay. Do not expect amenities akin to a starred hotel at Ashoka Grand, but the rooms are amply comfortable. You can order in-room dining.
Sagar Road, Shimoga; Ph: 08182-256086; www.ashokagrandshimoga.com; Tariff (excl. breakfast & taxes): ₹999–2,500.

GREEN VIEW BOUTIQUE
The hotel offers clean, spacious and airy rooms and a number of facilities and amenities to make the stay comfortable. Green View Boutique is an ideal budget stay if you're stopping over for a night and not looking for superior amenities.
Balraj Urs Road, Shimoga; Ph: 08182-273999; www.greenboutique.in; Tariff (double occupancy, incl. breakfast & taxes): ₹2,192–3,581.

ROYAL ORCHID CENTRAL
Decidedly the best stay in town, Royal Orchid is at par with top hotels with its superior facilities and amenities. Spacious rooms, in-house dining options and a large spread for breakfast are the highlights. It is used frequently by business travellers.
Opp. Vinayak Theatre, BH Road, Shimoga; Ph: 08182-409999; www.royalorchidhotels.com; Tariff: (double occupancy, incl. breakfast, excl. taxes): ₹3,600.

EATING OUT

It is recommended that you eat at the in-house dining options of the hotels mentioned.

HUBLI & DHARWAD

Often spoken in one breath, the twin towns of Hubli and Dharwad make for a good base en route to Dandeli. Largely a commercial set-up, there is little for tourists here, apart from the tranquil Unkal Lake and the Indira Gandhi Glass House Garden.

SIGHTSEEING HIGHLIGHTS
Unkal Lake
The serene lake is located on the outskirts of the city and offers a respite from the buzz of the city. It stands near the Chandramouleshwara Temple.

Timings: Sunrise to Sunset.

Chandramouleshwara Temple
The Chandramouleshwara Temple, a 900-year-old temple from the Badami Chalukyan era, is a masterpiece in design and architecture. It is a Shiva temple with a number of fascinating sculptures, other than the two Shivlingas and Nandi Bulls.

Timings: Sunrise to Sunset.

Nrupatunga Hill
A respite from the city, the Nrupatunga Hill offers sylvan views of the valley below. It is a popular hangout for locals who come up to beat the heat and traffic. The path up to the hill is flanked by lamp-posts, which are lit in the evenings. There is a children's park and a small restaurant on top.

Entry Fee: Adults: ₹10, Children: ₹5;
Timings: 11 a.m.–8.30 p.m.

Indira Gandhi Glass House Garden
The massive glasshouse is home to a number of different species of fauna. There is a musical fountain show, toy train ride for children and a flower show.

Sadashiv Nagar; Entry Fee: Free;
Timings: 7.30 a.m.–7.30 p.m.

DANDELI

A profusion of green hits you as soon as you enter Dandeli. Unarguably, Karnataka's most exciting rafting destination (on the Kali River), go there if you wear adventure on your sleeve. A number of waterfalls, the Anshi Dandeli Tiger Reserve and ancient caves and temples keep the tourist engaged for at least three days. It's a perfect setting for treks, nature walks and adventure activities.

SIGHTSEEING HIGHLIGHTS
Syntheri Rocks
You have to walk down 250 slippery steps to get a glimpse of the mammoth, near vertical, monolithic

Experience Karnataka

Swollen by the monsoon, Kaneri River gushes past Syntheri Rocks

300-feet-tall granite rock with the Kaneri River splashing at the base. Weathered by water and sun, the rock scape has a number of patterns and unique cave-like formations in it. The swollen-by-monsoon river is at its ferocious best. When the water level is low, one can go right upto the edge of the river.

Entry Fee: *Adults: ₹10, Children: ₹5; 2-wheeler: ₹10, 4-wheeler: ₹20;* **Timings**: *8.30 a.m.–5 p.m.*

Ulavi Channabasaveshwar Temple

Ulavi lies 63km from Dandeli town, but a trip here is worth your while. The temple is a pilgrimage centre for the Lingayat community of north Karnataka. Interesting sculptures inside depict common life rather than gods and goddesses. In the sanctum lies the *samadhi* (memorial) of Saint Channabasavanna.

Timings: *6 a.m.–8 p.m.*

RAFTING

White-water rafting on River Kali is the main reason why adventure lovers flock to Dandeli. Though started in the late 90s, it was in 2006 when the sport took the small town by storm, with weekends going packed with adventure enthusiasts. Unlike the other rafting destinations, which are active just before monsoons, Dandeli's season begins after the rains, from October to May.

You can experience up to Grade 3 plus rapids here on the 9.5km stretch from Ganesh Gudi to Maulangi. There are two slots to choose from: 9.30 a.m. and

Dandeli Wildlife Sanctuary

Enter the wildlife sanctuary of Dandeli region from the Pansoli gate. Arrive early or ask your accommodation to book a safari as only a limited number of jeeps (16) are allowed per day. One can only access the buffer zone of the total 845-sqkm park, but it is not uncommon to spot deer, elephants, gaur, bison and other mammals. The same stretch of the forest extends into Anshi, making the two regions part of the Anshi Dandeli Tiger Reserve. Though the months of April and May are the best for sighting, the park is open through the year.

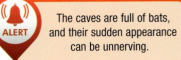

ALERT — The caves are full of bats, and their sudden appearance can be unnerving.

Pansoli; **Entry Fee:** *Indians: ₹400 (Adult), ₹200 (Children), Foreigners: ₹1,200 (Adult), ₹600 (Children);* **Timings***: 6–8 a.m., 4–6 p.m.;* **Trek***: ₹275 per head and ₹500 for a guide/group.*

Kavala Caves

Inaccessible during the rains, the Kavala Caves are a set of beautiful limestone stalagmite formations. The spot is 25km from Dandeli and you have to climb 375 steps down and further crawl into a narrow cave to see a natural Shivlinga. Carrying a torch is recommended.

Kali Tiger Reserve

Earlier called Anshi Tiger Reserve, the Anshi part of the protected forest area lies 52km from the Dandeli Wildlife Sanctuary's gate. The road leading to the 340-sqkm region is equally enchanting as the jungle itself. The safaris here are not operational, but trekking is possible. The Indian bison, wild boars, barking deer and many other mammals inhabit this region along with a fair population of reptiles and birds, including the great hornbill, Malabar pied hornbill,

---

2.30 p.m. Introduction, orientation and demonstration takes up 20 minutes before 7–9 people hop aboard the raft and start the 2-hour-long frothy journey along the river, interjected by eight rapids. Trained instructors who are equipped with helmets, life jackets, ropes and pro bags accompany each raft.

Each trip costs ₹1,400, inclusive of pick and drop (if you are coming in from Jungle Lodges Resort or Old Magazine), equipment and instruction. The age and weight limit for this activity is 15–60 years and below 100kg, respectively.

Dandeli; Ph: 09880131762; www.indiarafts.org

Experience Karnataka

▼ The backwaters reservoir of the Supa Dam makes it the third-biggest catchment area in the country

Malabar grey hornbill and Indian grey hornbill. If you are looking to experience camp life in this area, the Anshi Nature Camp is a decent facility.

Entry Fee: *Indians: ₹400 (Adults), ₹200 (Children), Foreigners: ₹1,200 (Adults), ₹600 (Children);* **Timings**: *6–8 a.m., 4–6 p.m.;* **Trek**: *₹275 per head and ₹500 for a guide/group.*

Supa Dam
The Supa Dam and its backwaters can be seen as soon as one enters Ganesh Gudi from Dandeli. Its reservoir is a massive sprawl of mirror-flat water, the third-biggest catchment area in the country. This is best viewed from a road bridge 10km from Ganesh Gudi.

The Vajra Waterfall makes a pretty sight

Vajra Waterfall
If you are going all the way to Anshi, an additional 3-km detour is valid to see the Vajra Waterfall. This is in its full glory during the rains. Stand and enjoy the spray by the edge of the road.

ACCOMMODATION

BISON RIVER RESORT
One of the oldest hotels on the banks of River Kali, Bison is an ideal pick for its access and view of the river. The first rapid of the Kali rafting stretch can be seen from here. Book the cottages closest to the river. Bison is the most popular resort for water-based and adventure activities.
Village Ambeli, Post Ganesh Gudi; Ph: 08383-256539; www.indianadventures.com; Tariff (incl. breakfast): ₹5,000 onwards (varies as per season).

CENTURY RESORT
Choose the rooms right next to the man-made water body in the property, which is the most scenic spot. The rooms look a little drab from outside but are plush from the inside. Dog lovers will especially like Century Resort for the in-house residents — a Labrador and a Great Dane.
Badhakanshirda; Ph: 09972151766; www.centuryresortdandeli.com; Tariff (incl. breakfast): ₹3,500–5,500.

HORNBILL RIVER RESORT
Choose the tree houses with the deck overlooking Kali River, which have large stable steps and well-maintained interiors. There is a choice of cottages too. Sprawling by the river, the Hornbill rafting experts are one of the two operators in the town.
Village Ambeli, Post Ganesh Gudi; Ph: 09880683323; www.hornbillriverresort.in; Tariff (incl. all meals & activities): ₹4,500 onwards, Tree house: ₹7,000 (varies as per season).

JUNGLE LODGES RESORT
Make an online booking to stay at the riverside property of Jungle Lodges, where you can choose to stay in atmospheric tents or rooms; the first-floor options, from where you can see the river, are recommended. The resort offers indoor games, rafting, safari in the jungle and nature walks with a naturalist. You can also check into a small five-roomed property called Old Magazine House by the same group — this is well known for birding.
Dandeli; Ph: 09449599795; www.junglelodges.com; Tariff (incl. all meals & activities): ₹4,610 onwards (tents), ₹4,948–5,666 per head (rooms).

KULGI NATURE CAMP
The oldest campsite and accommodation in the Dandeli region, this is the best way to enjoy the jungle ambience. The Kulgi Nature Camp lies close to Dandeli Wildlife sanctuary and offers luxury tents. Food is served in a common pavilion. A free interpretation centre and exhibits of local life in Dandeli, are adjacent to the campsite. The Kulgi Timber Trail lies next to the nature camp and has newer log huts. Booking for both these accommodations can be done at Dandeli Forest Office (Timings: 10 a.m.–5.30 p.m., Sundays & second Saturdays closed).
Kulgi; Ph: 08284-231585; Tariff: (incl. all meals): ₹2,000–2,400 (tents), ₹125 per head (dorms).

EATING OUT

There are no restaurants in Dandeli, save a few casual snack shops in the small market near the bus stand. Most resorts offer packages with meals.

SHOPPING

Dandeli is not known for shopping but Kaadumane offers the best of the local craft in a small shop in Potoli village. Women from 15 households produce masks made from lavancha grass, key chains and more. Warli painting is another theme used on bric-a-bracs. You can also find locally sourced squashes and honey here. Try the tropical speciality, kokum.
Timings: 10 a.m.–5 p.m.

History Unravelled

Rocky outcrops with patches of green are common in this belt

Badami ▶▶ Pattadakal ▶▶ Aihole ▶▶ Hampi

VITALS
Getting There
It would be ideal to use Badami as a base for the tri-city circuit of Pattadakal, Aihole and Badami since it has better travel infrastructure. Pattadakal and Aihole are 22km and 35km from Badami, respectively. Hubli is the closest airport from here at a distance of 106km. Pre-book a cab through your hotel at Badami for a pick up, as taxi service from the airport is not consistent. (₹2,000-3,000, depending on the car type). Badami has a small but fairly well-connected railway station. Hubli-bound trains from Bengaluru make a pit stop here; there are eight trains to choose from. Mumbai is also connected to the town by two trains. KSRTC (Karnataka State Road Transport Corporation) and private operators have overnight buses from Bengaluru.

Hiring a cab for a day will cost ₹1,500-2,000, depending on the car. Of course, if you're driving, the best way to cover this is by adding the historic town of Hampi with the sector. The entire route is a less than 250-km loop. If you're starting from Hampi, then take a train to Hospet, the nodal junction close by and reach the town by an auto (20-minute ride/₹200). Overnight KSRTC buses are also available.

Best Time to Go
The cooler months from October to February are ideal for this circuit, as the plains get extremely hot. The sun scorched temples and monuments are tough to walk on.

TOP TIP It's best to hire a car to explore the towns as local buses take longer routes and stop frequently, taking an hour more than the car.

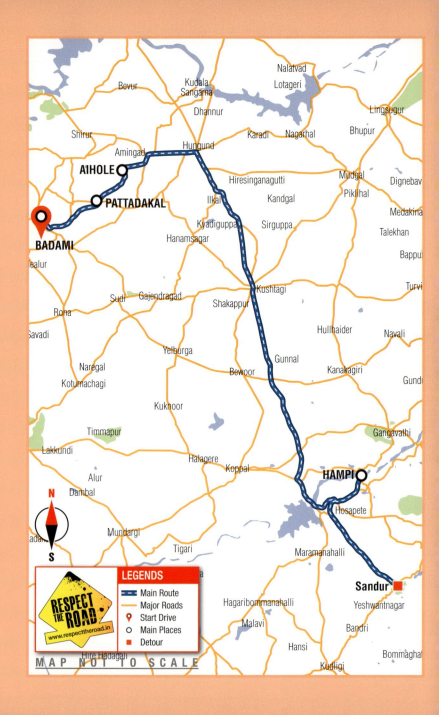

EXPLORING THE CIRCUIT

The loop of Vatapi (later Badami) and nearby towns of Pattadakal and Aihole, first conceived by the Chalukyas and further influenced by successors like Pallavas, Rashtrakutas, Kalyani Chalukyas, Yadavas, Kakatiyas, the Vijayanagar Empire, Adil Shah, Tipu Sultan and finally Aurangzeb for a few years, make for a history-filled trip. Of these five dynasties, the Chalukyas, Pallavas, Vijayanagar kings, Adil Shah and Tipu Sultan have left an imprint on the architectural styles on the many temples, which are the highlight of this trip.

Southwards, a gorgeous spectacle of boulder-strewn topography, dissected by a winding capillary, the Tungabhadra River, is what the Hampi scenery is largely made of. Transport yourself to at least 450 years ago when the ruling Vijayanagar kingdom was flourishing and elaborate temples – now in ruins – bore testimony to a time of grandeur. The spiritually inclined will love the adjacent village of Anegundi, the birthplace of Lord Hanuman. Detour to Sandur, an offbeat hamlet where tourism is low but a trip is worth your while for a stay in a palace, visiting ancient temples and watching the tribal women make magical products (bags and dresses) in bright colours.

BADAMI

SIGHTSEEING HIGHLIGHTS
Cave Temples

The meticulously numbered caves in the craggy rock face of Badami are the highlight of the town. Climb up to the four cave temples of

The imposing cave temples are made of deep red sandstone

Experience Karnataka

Badami from the foot of the South Fort. Made from deep red sand stones, the temples lie along a stepped pathway. Cave 1 is a Shiva temple with a detailed sculpture of an 18-armed dancing Shiva and an Ardhanarishvara avatar. Caves 2 and 3 are dedicated to Lord Vishnu where you can see the eight-armed icon of Vishnu sitting on Sheshnaag and the fierce lion-headed Narasimha. Also see the intricate carvings on the ceilings. Cave 4 is dedicated to the widely worshipped Jain Tirthankara, Mahavira. The South Fort is referred to a citadel, which was made by Tipu Sultan.

Entry Fee: Indians: ₹5, Foreigners: ₹100; **Video camera**: ₹25; **Car parking**: ₹15; **Timings**: 6 a.m.–6 p.m.

Agastya Lake

The prominent, green Agastya Lake is a man-made, stepped water body with an efficient drainage system, which keeps excessive rain water in check in the town. Besides providing the much-needed respite to the rising temperature of Badami, the water of the lake is also said to have healing powers. Smaller temples of Yellama, Virupaksha and Jambulinga lie at the edge of the lake.

The waters of Agastya Lake are said to have healing powers ▼

Bhutanatha Temples

Museum

The archaeological museum of Badami offers a collection of sculptures from Badami, Aihole and Pattadakal along with prehistoric exhibits found near Badami. A Pallava inscription can also be seen on a large boulder here. The museum falls on your route to Bhutanatha Temples and makes for a quick stop.

Entry Fee: Indians/Foreigners: ₹5;
Timings: 10 a.m.–5 p.m., Fridays closed.

Silidaphadi

Take a 3-km long walk from close to Badami bus stand to a natural rock shelter, which spans over 28 metres. The roof of this rock shelter is perforated in places, for light to come in – locals say it was possibly broken by lightning. Faint traces of prehistoric paintings can be found here. It is said that these belong to the first and second BC. Two other prehistoric sites, Ranganathgudda and Aralitirtha, can also be reached only on foot and are not recommended for elders and children.

Bhutanatha Temples

At the eastern edge of the Agastya Lake, there are two Bhutanatha Temples – one built in the sixth century and the other in the twelfth. The older temple is a Shiva shrine. The temples here are freestanding, without any mortar to hold the stones together; this is a feature you will see across the three towns. The Bhutanatha Temples is a great spot to relax and take in the grandeur of the Badami Caves from a distance.

Timings: 6 a.m.–6 p.m.

Experience Karnataka

Deep gorges in the North Fort area

North Fort

Be prepared for a steep climb of 200 metres above the lake area. A short distance from the arched entrance near the museum, you can reach the open *mandapas* (a pillared pavilion), and further on to the Lower and Upper Shivalayas (Shiva shrines). The climb is worth the effort for the panoramic view of the city and the caves on the opposite side. Another interesting monument here is the Malegitti Shivalaya, which is perched precariously on a massive boulder.

Timings: 6 a.m.–6 p.m.

> **ALERT**: This walk can take a long time and the sun can take a toll on you, even in the winters, so ensure that you visit here in the morning.

PATTADAKAL

SIGHTSEEING HIGHLIGHTS
Temple Complex

This is a world heritage site that was once the capital of the Chalukyan Empire. Shiva's imprint is certain in the temple complex of Pattadakal; the linga-strewn area gives away the prominent deity immediately. The Shiva shrines lie amidst well-kept lawns that are dominated by three major temples – Sangmeshwara, Virupaksha and Mallikarjuna. Of these, only the Virupaksha shrine is still an active temple, where *puja* (worshiping the deity) takes place daily. The other temples that lie here are the Jambulinga, Galaganatha, Kashivishvanatha and Kadasiddheshvara. All the temples face east and house intricate sculptures, stamped with stories inspired by the Mahabharata and Ramayana. What is fascinating to notice is that many craftsmen, who built these temples, have signatured somewhere on the sculptures.

Entry: Indians: ₹10, Foreigners: ₹250; *Video camera*: ₹25; *Timings*: 6 a.m.–6 p.m.

Papanatha Temple

The Papanatha Temple lies on the side of the main complex of Pattadakal and showcases a blend of the northern and southern styles of architecture. Stories from the Ramayana also unravel on the walls here.

Timings: 6 a.m.–6 p.m.

Jain Temple

Rather untreaded, another site of historical interest in Pattadakal is the Jain temple, just half a kilometre away from the main temple complex. The temple mostly exhibits style of the Rashtrakuta dynasty, with large elephant torsos sculpted in the walls – an instant sign of the kind of architecture adopted by the dynasty.

Timings: 6 a.m.–6 p.m.

▼ The neat temple complex in Pattadakal

AIHOLE

SIGHTSEEING HIGHLIGHTS
Megutii Hill
Start the trip to Aihole with the Meguti Hill early in the morning, to get a perspective and spread of the town that sprawls below. It's a short climb before you reach a double-storeyed Buddhist temple (with a headless statue of the Buddha). This is the only Buddhist temple in Aihole. Summit the hill to enter the AD 634-Jain temple. You can also see the ancient burial tombstones, dolmens, on the top of the hill. Climb down to visit the Mallikarjuna Complex with a simple shrine and a rock-cut Jain cave temple below.

Timings: 6 a.m.–6 p.m.

Durga Temple Complex
The main attraction of Aihole is the Durga Temple (though dedicated to Surya, which is a wonderful mix of Hindu and Buddhist-styles of architecture. The eighth-century temple has carvings of the Ramayana inside and masterpieces of Chalukyan architectural skills. Look out for larger-than-life sculptures of Shiva with Nandi, lion-headed Narasimha, Vishnu on Garuda and many more mythological icons that dot the complex. There is also a museum here with memorials dating back to the twelfth century. This gives one a great orientation into the history of the region.

Entry: Indians: ₹5, Foreigners: ₹100;
Camera: ₹25; *Video camera*: ₹25;
Timings: 6 a.m.–6 p.m., museum stays closed on Fridays.

The Durga Temple

ADDITIONAL STOPS FOR THE SPIRITUAL

Bathers in the Mahakuta Kalyani

Mahakuta
This lies 14km from Badami and is said to be connected to the city by a secretive, eucalyptus-lined, 3-km pathway, the gateway of which is flanked by skeletal figures of Kala and Kali. The main attraction of this walled complex is the Mahakuteshvar Temple and surrounding seventh-century shrines and a large tank fed by a natural spring. The place is abuzz with locals splashing in to beat the heat. Many tourists give this a miss, but the temple is a great stop to give yourself a rest from the elaborate Chalukyan theme of the circuit.

Banashankari Devi Temple
This lies only 5km from Badami, and holds great importance for pilgrims. It was built in the seventh century by Kalyani Chalukya kings, who worshipped Goddess Banashankari. The temple has used some of the late Chalukyan columns, but the most awe-inspiring feature is the lamp-studded tower at the temple. These are lit on special occasions. The annual festival, Banashankari Jatra, is held in the months of January or February.

Lad Khan Temple

Lad Khan is the name given to a temple that stands adjoining the main complex, after the man who inhabited it long after it was made. This is an eighth-century structure with a sloping roof and, from a distance, looks like it's been made from wooden panels. The temple columns inside are decorated with carvings and motifs.

Timings: 6 a.m.–6 p.m.

The Ravana Phadi Cave Temples have elaborate carvings

Ravana Phadi Cave Temples

One of the most interesting temples, this sixth-century temple has large sculptures of Ardhanarishvara, ten-armed Shiva and a scape of elaborate carvings around. Notice the sculptures of the gatekeepers at the entrance – they are depicted in Iranian dresses. This was possibly inspired from the travels of the ruling king and international interaction that he might have had.

Timings: 6 a.m.–6 p.m.

BE AWARE

ASI (Archaeological Survey of India) guides are available to hire in all major stops (₹1,000 for a group of 4). Chandru, who has been part of INTACH (Indian National Trust For Art and Cultural Heritage), and also taught at a small college in Badami, is recommended to accompany you. Well versed in English, he can modify his style based on your time and inclination to see the temples. You can contact him at 09448823161.

ROCK CLIMBING

Badami is a well-known rock-climbing destination. Bengaluru-based Mars Adventures organizes weekend trips (stay, food, equipment, instructions included) for beginners and pros to climb heights from 40–70 feet with top ropes. The routes are first thoroughly inspected by instructors before participants can start. Safety harness, helmet, chalk bag, quickdraws and crash mats are part of the equipment list so you know you're in good hands. Routes like 'Top Rope Gorge', 'Fire or Retire', 'French Disaster' and 'Hungry Climber' are the most popular.

No. 5 Kamakshi Nilaya, RM Nagar Main Road, Dodda Banaswadi, Bengaluru; Ph: 09886664666; www.marsadventures.in; Charges: ₹5,000 per head, onwards.

Rock climbing is a popular sport in Karnataka

ACCOMMODATION

THE HERITAGE RESORT
The best thing about this resort is the grassy patch in front of the rooms and a glorious view of the large rocky outcrop from the sit-out of your cottage. Well-furnished interiors, clean bathrooms and an in-house restaurant make The Heritage one of the best choices in Badami. Stay here if you want to stay clear of the clutter in the main town.

Station Road; Ph: 08357-220250; www.theheritage.co.in; Tariff: (AC, double occupancy, incl. breakfast): ₹2,500–3,200.

HOTEL BADAMI COURT
Badami Court is one of the oldest hotels of the town. The rooms are slightly snug and musty, but the triple-bed options are spacious and airy. Ask for the first-floor rooms overlooking the central garden, as they are better lit. The hotel also has an in-house restaurant, which is convenient.

173 Station Road; Ph: 08357-220230; Tariff: (double occupancy, incl. breakfast): ₹3,750–4,200.

HOTEL MAYURA CHALUKYA
Choose from the newly built wing of the hotel, rather than the old rooms. These are spacious

enough for 3 beds, so it's good for a family; there's a flat-screen TV, AC and a large clean bathroom. The state-tourism-run hotel is great value for money and also has an in-house restaurant.
Ramdurg Road, PWD Compound; Ph: 08357-220046; www.karnatakaholydays.net; Tariff (double occupancy, incl. breakfast): ₹1,850–2,200.

KRISHNA HERITAGE
This is the most convenient and luxurious address in town. Krishna Heritage is a short drive away from the bus stand and offers luxury cottages with modern amenities. The decor is minimalistic and soothing. The hotel also has a semi open-air in-house restaurant, a travel desk and 24-hour room service, which is always welcome after a tired day of sightseeing. The hotel can also help with pick up and drop, and sightseeing tours.
Ramdurg Road; Ph: 08357-221300; www.krishnaheritagebadami.com; Tariff (double occupancy, incl. breakfast): ₹3,500.

EATING OUT

There are not too many options of restaurants in Badami, so it's best to stick to the in-house dining options of the hotels.

BANASHRI HOTEL
The restaurant serves both north and south Indian food. It's a good option for a no-frills, quick meal, though you may have to jostle for space to sit.
Opp. KSRTC Bus Stop, Main Road; Ph: 09916259676; Meal for 2: ₹250–500; Timings: 6.30 a.m.–10.30 p.m.

KRISHNA BHAVAN
If you are up for a local veg meal (Lingayat Khanavali) of jowar rotis, rice and spicy local curries, enter here. You won't be disappointed.
Main Road; Ph: 09845277748; Meal for 2: Below ₹250; Timings: 10 a.m.–10 p.m.

SHOPPING

The Ilkal saris and fabrics of the region are well known. You could visit **Shri Shiddalingeshwara Javali & Cloth Stores** to buy a sari or fabrics. This establishment has been running their own looms since the last forty years and is a great option to find a large variety of Ilkal specials ranging from ₹300–5,000. Iconic *pallus* in silk and cotton can be seen. You can also request to see the looms and see the weavers in action (30km from Badami).
Main Road; Ph: 09480535310; Timings: 9.30 a.m.–9 p.m., Sundays closed.

Hampi is famous for its architectural ruins and shrines (above and below)

HAMPI

Hampi lies 148km south of Badami. Several strong religious and historic themes are a highlight – a strong religious sentiment towards Lord Hanuman since he was born in Anegundi, an adjacent village; the historic perspective with ruins of the ancient Vijayanagar kingdom; and a Bohemian hippie vibe that has brought in a veritable Western backpacking influence.

It is important to understand the different important areas of Hampi. The main street leading from the Virupaksha Temple of Hampi, the Virupapur Gaddi (better known as the 'other side of the river') and the adjoining village of Anegundi make the three central regions to discover in Hampi. It is the fascinating monument trail that tourists come to see. Other than that, the highlight is the Anegundi village run by the Kishkinda Trust and the Daroji Sloth Bear Sanctuary.

Experience Karnataka

ALERT: It is vital that you remember the strict timings of the boat/ferry, as getting stuck on either side would mean a trek of 40km by auto by a different route.

You can stay in Virupapur Gaddi (also known as Hampi Island), which has cheap and clean guesthouses with better access to food and beer. Hampi Street and Virupapur Gaddi are separated by the Tungabhadra River where two boats ply between 7 a.m. and 6 p.m. to ferry people across (**Fare**: Indians: ₹15, Foreigners: ₹20).

SIGHTSEEING HIGHLIGHTS
Monument Trail

Hampi and its adjoining regions are dotted with ASI-maintained monuments from the Vijayanagar kingdom of AD 1500. Though basic information is given on boards outside the important temples, it is best to see these with guides. There are about 83 marked monuments and plenty of others in the vicinity – all of which have been declared a World Heritage Site by UNESCO. The key ones are mentioned below.

MATHANGA PARAVATH

The Mathanga Paravath stands right opposite the Virupaksha Temple at the far end of the street – a small hill that is excellent to climb for stunning views below. Irregular grassy steps lead up to this hill, with a Veerabhuvneshwara shrine to look out for at the summit. It takes about 30 minutes to trek up. The sunrise view is recommended.

QUEEN'S BATH

Ornate windows hang over a central bathing pool, immediately

Queen's Bath is a popular site among tourists

The Virupaksha Temple sees a crowd of devotees every day

depicting the extravagance in daily life of the queens of the erstwhile kingdom. The Queen's Bath is one of the most atmospheric monuments of the trail.

Hampi; **Timings**: *8 a.m.–5.30 p.m.*

MAHANAVAMI DIBBA

A relief from many elaborate temples, this structure is built most plainly, like a plateau. The Vijayanagar king, Krishnadevaraya built this 22-feet high platform to celebrate a win over Orissa. A geometrically designed *kalyani* (bathing pool), which lies in the same complex, is the highlight.

Hampi; **Timings**: *8 a.m.–5.30 p.m.*

VIRUPAKSHA TEMPLE

This Shiva temple is synonymous to the postcard image of Hampi. A small 'bazaar' street stretches in front of this, ending in a large monolithic Nandi Bull facing the temple on the other end. Virupaksha is an active temple with plenty of devotees visiting each day. Apart from seeing the intricate ceiling paintings and manoeuvring through the monkey-infested paths, keep your eyes peeled for an interesting natural pinhole camera image of the tower inside the complex.

Hampi Bazaar, Hampi; **Entry Fee**: ₹2; **Timings**: *6 a.m.–8 p.m.*

Experience Karnataka

This temple, dedicated to Lord Rama, was built by King Devaraya I in the 15th century

VIJAYA VITALLA TEMPLE
The iconic chariot that one sees in many visuals of Hampi was built in 1513, as part of the temple dedicated to Lord Vishnu. The Vijaya Vitalla Temple is known as an architectural marvel for its musical pillars and workmanship. The chariot, inspired by the one in Konark, was actually functional till it was cemented in by the authorities. The long pathway to the temple can now be crossed in battery-operated vehicles, driven mostly by women (**Fare**: ₹20).

Hampi Bazaar, Hampi; **Entry Fee**: *Indians:* ₹*10, Foreigners:* ₹*250;* **Timings**: *6 a.m.–8 p.m.*

LOTUS MAHAL & ELEPHANT STABLES
The distinct look of this monument is given away by the blend of Hindu- and Muslim-architectural styles. The Lotus Mahal is flanked by well-maintained gardens. Further from the same gate, 11 dome-shaped stables stand. These were constructed for the royal elephants.

Hampi Bazaar, Hampi; **Entry Fee**: *Indians:* ₹*10, Foreigners:* ₹*250;* **Timings**: *6 a.m.–8 p.m.*

ACHYUTARAYA TEMPLE
The Achyutaraya Temple is dedicated to Lord Vishnu. Marked by its pillared walkway, which can be distinctly seen from the Mathanga Parvath, the pillars have carvings from the Mahabharata and Ramayana. Other features include a wide bazaar street and *kalyana mandapa* (marriage hall) like many other temples built in that age.

Hampi; **Timings**: *8 a.m.–5.30 p.m.*

Anegundi
The village of Anegundi lies on the opposite side of the Tungabhadra River and is also home to a number of ruins, primarily the elephant stables, Pampa Sarovar Temple, the Sanapur Reservoir, ancient cave paintings, the village library and Chintamani Temple. Maintained by the Kishkinda Trust, the village deserves a whole day to discover. The main thing to see here is the Anjandri Hill. Arrive early at the foot of this hill to beat the sun and trek up to the birthplace of Lord Hanuman, which is infested by monkeys. More than 600 well-

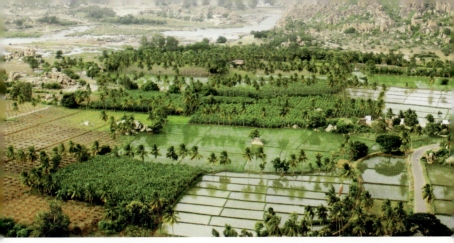

View from Anjandri Hill, Anegundi. Below: View of the thousand *lingas* from a coracle ride

constructed steps lead up to this simple shrine. The view of Anegundi village and the monuments across the river, from the Anjandri Hill is jaw-droppingly beautiful.

Timings: *Sunrise to Sunset.*

Daroji Sloth Bear Sanctuary

Located 17km away from Hampi town, the Daroji Sloth Bear Sanctuary is a clean and well-maintained home to 120 sloth bears amongst other animals. The bears are fed at about 2 p.m., so it's best to get to the watchtower and see them from relatively closer proximity. Binoculars are helpful. One can also drive inside to the viewing point in your own vehicle.

Daroji Sloth Bear Sanctuary, Kamlapura; **Entry Fee**: *Adults:* ₹50, *Children:* ₹25, *Foreigner:* ₹300; **Camera**: ₹300; **Timings**: *1.30 p.m.–6 p.m.*

CORACLE RIDES

A coracle ride is an imperative addition to the list of things to do in Hampi. There are two points in Hampi from where coracles run from; one is near the Kodanda Rama Temple and the other, Talwarkatta in Anegundi. It gives one an opportunity to see rock formations on the banks of the river, otherwise inaccessible by foot. If you are starting from the Kodanda Rama side, ask to see the thousand *lingas* and sleeping Vishnu sculptures on the rocks. Depending on the duration of the ride, it can cost you anywhere between ₹50–250 per head. Bargain well.

Experience Karnataka

ACCOMMODATION

ART RESIDENCY, ANEGUNDI
Earthy cottages with cement beds and colourful cotton furnishings are the main aesthetics of Art Residency. The leaf imprints on the floor and balconies overlooking a central grassy patch add to the charm. Choose the triple deluxe suite if you are travelling with family. With an extra bed, this will be perfect.
G.R.O.W. Pvt. Ltd., Registered Branch Office, Survey No. 207, Talwarkatta Road, Anegundi; Ph: 09449972230; Tariff (double occupancy): ₹5,000 onwards.

BOULDERS, HAMPI
The only non-backpacking option in Hampi to stay, Boulders should be the choice if you are looking for a super-luxury holiday. Spacious sit-outs offer undisturbed views of River Tungabhadra, flowing right beside the property. The nature trail offered is packed with stunning rock formations and a vantage deck set up on a cave.
Narayanpet, Bandi Harlapura Munirabad, Koppal District; Ph: 09242641551; www.hampisboulders.com; Tariff (double occupancy, incl. full board): ₹10,000.

GOAN CORNER
Stay by the riverside with a view of the bright green paddy fields, and laze on the hammocks that swing outside each room. Goan Corner promises an easy-paced vibe to your holiday, with a fuss-free, but basic stay.
Virupapur Gaddi; Ph: 08533287002; Tariff (double occupancy): ₹1,000 onwards.

GOWRI RESORT
Away from the bustle and touristy clutter, escape to Gowri Resort in Sanapur. The basic, shack-like property faces bright green fields and a bouldery sprawl. The sit-outs with a swing are the best part of the property, as is the fact that you are away from the main hub.
Sanapur; Ph: 09449663611; Tariff (double occupancy): ₹1,000 onwards.

HEMA GUEST HOUSE, HAMPI
One of the most popular and clean set-ups in Virupapur Gaddi, go there for the splash of colour that hits you in the form of bright cloth hammocks outside each room. Orthodox Jewish visitors are bound to feel more comfortable as a separate area is set up for Friday prayers with traditional food for them exclusively. The guesthouse operates between September–April.
Virupapur Gaddi, Hampi; Ph: 09449103008; Tariff (double occupancy): ₹500–1,000 (depending on season).

HERITAGE RESORT, HAMPI
This is one of the newer options off Hampi town and one that promises luxury – think pool, Jacuzzi in the cottage and garden villas. The property is in tune with the earthy colours of Hampi and has a soothing ambience. It is well equipped with an in-house restaurant, spa, pool and other activities.
State Highway 49; Ph: 080-25232329;- www.indoasia-hotels.com; Tariff (double occupancy, incl. breakfast, dinner & taxes): ₹7,700.

MOWGLI GUEST HOUSE, HAMPI
A combination of few AC and non-AC basic rooms either face the lush paddy fields or the courtyard at Mowgli Guest House. A mosquito net is the only additional facility provided in the room. The lounge-cum-dining area has floor seating and great food – perfect to get lazier by the hour.
Virupapur Gaddi, Hampi; Ph: 09448003606; www.mowglihampi.com; Tariff (double occupancy): ₹900-1,200 (depending on season).

PESHEGAAR HOUSE, ANEGUNDI
Five basic and clean rooms in a local house make

a great option to be oriented to the local life of Anegundi. The bathrooms are on sharing basis, but it's not an impediment at all.
G.R.O.W. Pvt. Ltd., Registered Branch Office, Survey No. 207, Talwarkatta Road, Anegundi; Ph: 09449972230; Tariff (double occupancy): ₹800 onwards.

ROYAL ORCHID CENTRAL, HOSPET
This is definitely the best luxury option in Hospet. The hotel has all essential amenities like swimming pool, spa and gymnasium.
Station Road, Hospet; Ph: 08394-300100; www.royalorchidhotels.com; Tariff (double occupancy): ₹4,500 onwards.

SHANTHI GUEST HOUSE, HAMPI
Shanthi Guest House has largely led the aesthetics for other guesthouses on the Virupapur Gaddi since 1992. Thatched or concrete rooms with a mosquito net and a swing outside either look out into the garden or the paddy fields are available. The guesthouse also has an in-house travel desk and can arrange for sightseeing with local guides.
Virupapur Gaddi, Hampi; Ph: 09449260162; www.shanthihampi.com; Tariff (double occupancy): ₹800-1,500 (depending on season).

SRI KRISHNA INN, HOSPET
The rooms are clean and well equipped, though slightly musty smelling. A gym, swimming pool and Internet facilities are unanticipated in this small town and, therefore, a pleasant surprise.
Station Road, Hospet; Ph: 08394-294321; www.krishnapalacehotel.com; Tariff (double occupancy): ₹4,000 onwards.

URAMMA, ANEGUNDI
The beautiful high ceilings, stone pillars, red walls and warm furnishings of Uramma are delightful. It's difficult to imagine this plush an option as it is in the heart of Anegundi village. The house has only two rooms (preferably given to a single group). Uninterrupted power supply and Wi-fi are extra perks.
G.R.O.W. Pvt. Ltd, Registered Branch Office, Survey No. 207, Talwarkatta Road, Anegundi; Ph: 09449972230; Tariff (for 4 people): ₹15,000.

EATING OUT
All the guesthouses in Virupapur Gaddi have cafés with floor seating and great Continental menus.

BHUVNESHWARI SELF HELP GROUP
There is no better way to get a bite of local life – quite literally. Anegundi women's self-help group dishes out the best Jowar and Bajra Rotis served with seven chutneys and dal. This simple fare tastes even better over a quick chat with the ladies. This needs to be organized with prior notice.
G.R.O.W. Pvt. Ltd, Registered Branch Office, Survey No. 207, Talwarkatta Road, Anegundi; Ph: 09449972230; Meal for 2: Below ₹500.

MANGO TREE, HAMPI
The popular haunt of Hampi, the Mango Tree restaurant, lies in the main market on the Virupaksha Temple side. This was shifted from a coveted spot by the river to this location, but still continues to be the best place for a meal. Floor mats are perfect to laze in and order from a vast menu of Indian, Continental and Israeli cuisines. The Egg Curry and Roti Combo, downed with a glass of Mango Lassi is perfect to start a lazy afternoon here.
Hampi; Ph: 09448765213; Meal for 2: ₹200–500; Timings: 7.30 a.m.–9.30 p.m.

SHOPPING

CLOTHES & JEWELLERY
In tune with its Boho vibe, Hampi is dotted with small shack-like shops for clothes and jewellery. You can find flowing harem pants, string tops and such on the other side of the river. These shops were earlier lined adjacent to Virupaksha Temple but have found a new home in the area they truly belong to.

HANDICRAFTS, BHOOMI SOCIETY
Started by the Kishkinda Trust, the Bhoomi Society is now a self-sustained establishment, which employs over 200 women in creating products from natural fibres of banana, water hyacinth and river grass. One can visit the workshop in Anegundi to pick well-crafted baskets, tablemats and file bags.
Next to Gram Panchayat Office, Off Chariot Street; Ph: 08533-267793; Timings: 10 a.m.–5 p.m. (lunch break: 1-2 p.m.).

DETOUR
Sandur

Situated 42km from Hampi, the small village of Sandur is wedged between iron-rich low mountains of Bellary district and surrounded by lush countryside. Sandur, once a princely state ruled by the Ghorpade family, promises transporting you to an era of kings and grand palaces. Erstwhile Skandapuri, this was known as the city of Skanda or Kumaraswamy, whose temple still gazes down at the town from the top of a hill close by. Till now, the edge of the town mingles with vast tracts of cornfields and a ludicrous amount of green and is skirted by mountains in the distance. For tourists, this is the perfect retreat from the urban world. In fact, Mahatma Gandhi himself, called Sandur 'an oasis' when he visited in the 1930s.

Stay at the Shivavilas Palace, now a WelcomHeritage property. With royal suites, excellent hospitality and superior amenities, this is sure to offer a great holiday.

Palace Road, Sandur; Ph: 08395260223; www.welcomheritagehotels.in; Tariff (AC, double occupancy, incl. breakfast): ₹2,500–3,200.

Apart from the palace itself, it's the places around that draw in a tourist. Two of the most important places are mentioned below.

KUMARASWAMY TEMPLE

A short ride from Shivavilas Palace, through the curves of the iron-rich mountains lies the 1,200-year-old ancient temple of Kumaraswamy (Lord Karthikeya). The drive to the temple is accompanied by corn and banana fields. Once you reach the top, you can see that the weathered walls still tell lores of the dynasties that ruled the region and left an indelible mark on the culture of the area since then. The temple was constructed by the Chalukyas and further reconstructed by the Rashtrakutas. Earlier, women were not allowed in the temple, but the ban was lifted by Maharaja Murarirao Yeshwantrao Ghorpade of the Sandur Palace, further propelling him to a place of great reverence amongst the locals.

Inside the main sanctum, the gold-plated eyes on the black stone statue add to Lord Kumaraswamy's gaze. On either side of the main temple lie shrines made for his parents, Lord Shiva and Parvati.

Timings: 6 a.m.–Noon, 2–7.30 p.m.; Distance/time: 13km/45 minutes; the palace can provide a map for self-driving guests.

SANDUR KUSHALA KALA KENDRA

Another establishment that is supported by the palace deserves a few hours from tourists. Here, you get to see the brilliant handicraft work by the Lambani (nomadic) tribal women of north Karnataka. Started in 1984, SKKK (Sandur Kushala Kala Kendra) touches base with 350 local artisans and craftsmen who are employed for traditional embroidery and mirror work, cane craft, woodwork and stone sculpting. The women-focused Kendra is a hectic place with a number of women on tailoring machines, while others sit and create magic in mirrors and colourful threads to make bags, garments, home furnishings, jewellery and accessories.

Timings: 10 a.m.–1 p.m., 3–5.30 p.m., Sundays closed; Distance/time: 1.5km/10 minutes.

Stories in Stone

The Madrasa built by Mohamad Gawan. Photo: Lakshmi Prabhala

Vijayapura ▸▸ Bidar

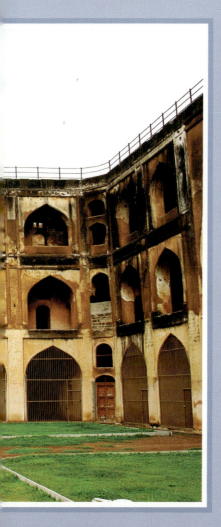

VITALS
Getting There
Vijayapura (formerly Bijapur) is one of the most architecturally stunning cities in Karnataka. Wedged in the basalt rock topography of the northeastern part of the state, it has a distinct vibe to it. The city lies at a distance of over 500km from the capital, Bengaluru, and is best accessed by train. There are ten options that one can choose from; NH4 and NH13 cut across the heart of the state, in case one wants to drive all the way from Bengaluru. Overnight state-run and private buses are also available. It is best to drive between Vijayapura and Bidar so you can halt at Basavakalyan in the middle and also flit easily between the many monuments that lie in each city.

Best Time to Go
The cooler months from October to February are ideal for this circuit, as the rocky topography gets extremely hot.

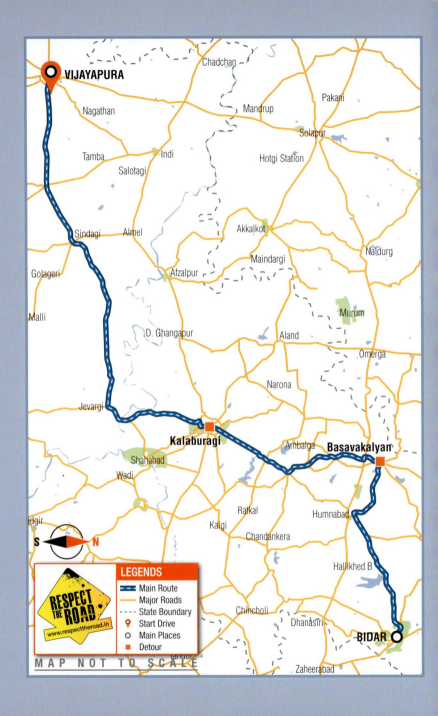

EXPLORING THE CIRCUIT

The enchanting remnants of the Adil Shah dynasty casts a spell on the tourist. Start the drive from Vijayapura, the city of victory, which was established by the Chalukyas in the tenth century. It later moved hands to the Yadavas and then the Khilji Sultanate in the thirteenth century. The highlights of Vijayapura include the stunning Gol Gumbaz, the largest dome in India. Other architectural delights are also cut out from the basalt rock and have traces of Mughal influences.

A drive of over 300km northeast from Vijayapura lies the hilltop town of Bidar. It lies on the edge of the adjoining state of Telangana. The Bidar Fort, an awe-inspiring network of water channels (Karez system), one of the holiest gurudwaras for the Sikhs and the second-largest air force base of the country gives one ample reason to visit here. Add to that the fine *bidri* handicraft and you can easily spend a couple of days here.

VIJAYAPURA

SIGHTSEEING HIGHLIGHTS
Ibrahim Rouza

Ibrahim Adil Shah, who ruled between 1580 and 1627, was one of the most tolerant leaders of the era. The Ibrahim Rouza is his tomb. With well-defined symmetric features, many suspect that it was the inspiration behind the Taj Mahal. So much so, that the moniker of 'Taj Mahal of the Deccan' has been imprinted in the minds of tourists. The structure comprises a mosque and a tomb which lie astride, only divided by a fountain in the middle. The green lawns around the buildings further accentuate the bleached brown hues of the structures.

Entry: ₹10; Timings: 6 a.m.–6 p.m; Fridays closed.

Malik-E-Maidan

This seventeenth-century largest-medieval canon of the world is worth a trip for. Malik-E-Maidan, the 55-ton canon was brought back as a trophy of war from Ahmednagar. It was presented by a Turkish officer who served Burhan Nizamshah. The canon lies in front of the Gol Gumbaz.

Upli Burj

The 80-feet tall tower was built in 1584. Upli Burj has spiral steps running inside, while the top of the tower offers arresting views of the city below. Possibly used as a monitoring tower, the top also had two guns.

Timings: Sunrise to Sunset.

Gol Gumbaz

The tomb of Mohammed Adil Shah, who ruled the region in the

The Gol Gumbaz has become synonymous with Vijayapura. Photo: Anuradha Goyal

fifteenth century, is the most iconic structure of the city. It boasts the largest dome in India and is only second to the dome of St Peter's Basilica in Rome. The cube-like structure with the dome top has several other interesting features: the whispering gallery where a mere whisper is amplified to be heard 37 metres away; four minarets on the corners; a mosque; a *naqqar khana* (hall for trumpeters); and some additional ruins that dot the manicured garden around it.

Entry Fee: ₹2; **Timings**: 10 a.m.–5 p.m.; Fridays closed.

Chand Bawdi

A tank that was built during the rule of Ali Adil Shah, Chand Bawdi could store over 20 million litres of water. Named after his wife, Chand Bibi, a grand complex surrounded the stepped tank and was used as residential quarters for the staff of the royal family.

Timings: Sunrise to Sunset.

Asar Mahal

The Hall of Justice was built by Adil Shah in the mid-fifteenth century. It has majestic wooden columns and a wooden ceiling; the walls and ceilings both have paintings. Decorated by delicate frescos and a tank in the complex, the hall is the venue for an annual Urs festival. The structure also has a mosque where women are not allowed.

Timings: Sunrise to Sunset.

Jami Masjid

One of the oldest mosques in the Deccan, Jami Masjid was built by Adil Shah when he won the Vijayanagar kingdom in the south. An open court is surrounded by two wings, encasing a large area of 1,16,300 sqft. Notice the *mehrab*, which is painted aesthetically, and the pavilion, which is ascribed to Aurangzeb.

Saath Kabar

A rather dark legend surrounds Saath Kabar. It is believed that an army chief, Afzal Khan, who killed his 63 wives fearing they would remarry after his death, buried them here. This is just before he set out to fight the great Maratha warrior, Shivaji.

Gagan Mahal

Another poignant structure, this is the place where Sikandar Adil Shah surrendered to Aurangzeb in 1681. Gagan Mahal (Sky Palace) has a 2-metre facade and three majestic arches. The central arch is the widest of the three. It was built as a royal palace, and also has a durbar hall, which is now in ruins.

DETOUR
Kalaburagi

Located 165km from Vijayapura, Kalaburagi (earlier Gulbarga) is known for a number of monuments, including the tomb of Bahamani Sultan Hasan, Government Museum, Ferozabad Fort, Sharanabasaveshwar Temple, Sri Kshetra Ganagapur (Ganagapur), Sri Hulakantheshwar Temple, the Ghathargi Bhagavanti Temple on the bank of the Bhima River and the Bahamani Fort. Keep two days for this city or pick and choose what you want to see before heading in the direction of Bidar.

Basavakalyan

Named after Vishwaguru Basavanna, a revolutionary who established Anubhava Mantapa (spiritual democracy) in twelfth-century India, Basavakalyan makes for a quick stop. It has the world's tallest statue of Basavanna at 108 feet. Since the city went through a vibrant lineage of Chalukyas to the nizams, the monuments are equally interesting and reflect a varied past. The primary highlights are Jalasangvi, Narayanapura and Shivapura temples of the Chalukya dynasty, the Basaveshwara Temple and monuments like Moti Mahal, Hydari Mahal and Peeran Durga that have an Islamic heritage. And other religious places such as Gachchina Matha, Kambali Matha and Sadananda Matha.

ACCOMMODATION

HOTEL KANISHKA INTERNATIONAL
Expect basic facilities in Kanishka International hotel. Access to the centre of town and sightseeing spots is one of the reasons to stay here. There is an in-house restaurant on the property. The rooms are spacious and clean.
Station Road; Ph: 0835-2223788; www.kanishkabijapur.com; Tariff (double occupancy, excl. breakfast & taxes): ₹1,300–3,200.

HOTEL MADHUVAN INTERNATIONAL
Clean rooms, room service and a large outdoor garden are the draw for Madhuvan International hotel. It lies on Station Road, offering easy access to the monuments.
Ph: 0835-255571; Station Road; Tariff (double occupancy, excl. breakfast & taxes): ₹1,300–3,200.

EATING OUT

It is best to eat at the hotel where one is staying for more hygienic food. Small joints in the market are available, but are unexceptional.

BIDAR

Known as the city of whispering monuments, Bidar lies wedged on the northeastern edge of the state, sharing a boundary with neighbouring Telangana. The 500-year-old fort and some other interesting historical features of the city make it a veritable spot to visit. Sultan Alla-Ud-Din Bahman of the Bahamanid dynasty built the city. More recently, the fort has been the backdrop for many Bollywood movies, making it an interesting highlight for tourists.

SIGHTSEEING HIGHLIGHTS
Bahamani Tombs
A group of 12 tombs located in Ashtoor are worth your while. The large serene tombs have lofty tops and grand arches.

Gurudwara Nanak Jhira Sahib
One of the most important pilgrimages for Sikhs, the gurudwara commemorates a visit of Guru Nanak during a famine. The Gurudwara Nanak Jhira Sahib was established in 1948.

Bidar Fort
Considered one of the most formidable forts in the country, it overlooks the rest of the city. The fort is a jaw-droppingly stunning symbol of the Bahamani dynasty and was built by Sultan Alla-Ud-Din Bahman. It was constructed in the Persian-style

The Bidar Fort has many buildings, pavilions and *mahals* within the complex

of architecture. The Bidar Fort has five prominent gates, and two additional ones that are unnamed.

Mahals of Bidar

Though much of the fort city lies in ruins, parts of it still hold the remnants of a graceful past. Colourful tiles, carvings inlaid with mother of pearl and sculptures adorn the walls of the many smaller complexes around the fort. Of these, the *mahals* (palaces) are the most exquisite.

RANGEEN MAHAL
Situated near the fort, the palace Rangeen Mahal is a brilliant depiction of woodwork and mother of pearl usage, which was the highlight of that era. Delicate floral patterns and stone carvings are worth a trip here.

TAKHT MAHAL
An erstwhile royal residence, the walls of Takht Mahal are decorated with stone carvings and coloured tiles.

Experience Karnataka

KAREZ SYSTEM

The historic water supply system in Bidar, also known as *qanat*, was brought to Bidar in the fifteenth century by the Bahamani kings. A technique that originated in Persia, it is a network of underground canals to tap on the water and vertical shafts on the surface. Given the rocky topography of Bidar, water was sparse and this water was used from irrigation to household usage. The canals can still be seen till date, though they are not in use.

TARKASH MAHAL

It is believed that Tarkash Mahal was the palace for a Turkish wife of the sultan. Later, during the leadership of the Barid Shahi sultans, it was a harem. The ornamentation on the walls of the palace is beautiful.

▲ The remnants of the Tarkash Mahal

Chaukhandi
A stunning tomb dedicated to honour Hazrat Khalil Ullah, the spiritual adviser of Ahmad Shah, Chaukhandi stands about 4km from the fort.

Chaubara
An erstwhile watchtower, the 22-metre-high cylindrical tower is a great place to climb to and get a bird's eye view of the town.

ACCOMMODATION

BLACKBUCK RESORT
Located 18km from Bidar, the Jungle Lodges property has a rustic vibe to it, given that it is tucked between the Honnikeri Reserve Forest and the Vilaspur Lake. Go there to unwind and unplug from city life and watch blackbucks roaming free in the grasslands. This one is ideal for wildlife enthusiasts. There are 18 cottages to choose from in the property.
Vilaspur; Ph: 080 22111401; www.blackbuckresort.com; Tariff (double occupancy, full board with activities, excl. taxes): ₹4,078–5,078 per head.

There are a handful of other budget options to stay, but Blackbuck Resort is an ideal choice.

EATING OUT

It is best to eat at the hotel itself as Bidar has only modest restaurants in the market.

SHOPPING

BIDRIWARE
The metal handicraft from Bidar was originally imported from Persia during the reign of the Bahamani kings. Bidriware is the name given to metalwork, which uses an alloy of zinc and copper inlaid with fine sheets of silver. Pots, curios, spoons, *paan* (a preparation using betel leaf, areca nut and other ingredients that is eaten after a meal) holders, bowls and earrings are only few of the many things that the artisans make. Visit Kusum Galli in Bidar where you are likely to find a number of stores and artisans at work.

Experience **Karnataka**

TEMPLE TRAIL *for the* SPIRITUALLY INCLINED

For the spiritually inclined, Karnataka offers numerous ancient shrines. This trail maps the five temples that one should include if legends, mythology and spectacular architecture add up to amplifying a trip.

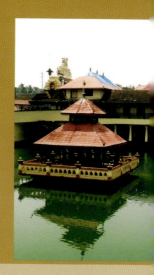

SRI MANJUNATHA SWAMY TEMPLE, DHARAMSTHALA

Dharamsthala lies off the Bangalore–Mangalore Highway (NH48), with the meandering Netravati River as a backdrop. Compared to other temples, there are no intricate carvings inside the sanctum of this Shiva (Sri Manjunatheshwara) and Parvathi (Shiva's consort Ammanavaru) shrine. The most fascinating part of the temple is that more than 10,000 devotees are offered free meals every day by a troupe of kitchen staff.

Timings: 6.30 a.m.–2 p.m., 7–8.30 p.m.

SRI MOOKAMBIKA DEVI, KOLLUR

Dedicated to Trishakti (Shakti or Parvathi, Saraswathi and Maha Lakshmi), the ancient temple of Mookambika lies in Kollur on the edge of Kerala. The town lies on the banks of River Souparnika, 27km from Byndoor on the western coast of Karnataka. The idol of Sri Mookambika in the sanctum is in the form of a Jyotir-Lingam, which means that it incorporates both features of Shiva and Parvathi. This is also one of the seven Mukti Sthalas created by the mythological character Parashurama.

Timings: *5 a.m.–2 p.m., 3–9 p.m.*

SRI SHARADA PEETHAM, SRINGERI

This abode of Goddess Sharadamba (Saraswathi) was established by Adi Shankaracharya himself. It was here on the idyllic banks of River Tunga that he

also set up the first of his four *maths* (religious centres) in India. The current *acharya*, Jagadguru Shankaracharya Sri Sri Bharati Tirtha Mahaswamiji, lives here and gives daily *darshan* to the devotees. This *peetham* (holy site) is the stronghold of Advaita learning of the Sanatan Dharma.

Timings: 6 a.m.–2 p.m., 5–9 p.m.

SRI SAMSTHANA MAHABALESHWARA DEVA, GOKARNA
The *atmalingam* (self-manifested, or created on its own) at this Shiva temple invokes zealous devotion that lies at the edge of the Arabian Sea. Replete with legends, the temple is often given the moniker of 'Kashi Vishwanath of South India'. A mere glimpse of the sanctum is said to bestow countless blessings.

Timings: 6 a.m.–12.30 p.m., 5–8 p.m.

SRI KRISHNA MATH, UDIPI
'Parasuram Kshetra' is the name given to one of the most famous temples in Karnataka. The breathtaking idol of Lord Krishna can be seen through a small metal window in the sanctum. The legendary lore of Sage Madhvacharya dreaming of the idol and then consecrating it here, keeps the interest of the devotees high. It is famous for the Paryaya festival that happens once in two years.

Timings: 5–9 p.m.

FOOD of KARNATAKA on a MAP

Karnataka not only offers a variety of travel experiences but it's also rich in the spread of cuisines across the state. You're likely to see subtle and sometimes distinct differences in each district, and influences from adjoining states. For the foodie, Kannada cuisine is one of the most exhilarating in India. On this map, you will find the highlights of different towns.

UNAVOIDABLE FOOD PIT STOPS ALONG THE COAST

The NH4 that runs along the west coast of Karnataka is one of the most scenic drives of India. The road also provides for ample pit stops for foodies, ensuring that you get an orientation of the different specialities along the highway. Here are a few of the most iconic restaurants and *dhabas* that warrant a stop.

1. HOTEL SADANAND, SURATHKAL
Stop here to savour the traditional coastal cuisine. Choose the basement section for a non-fuss atmosphere and quick service. Regulars recommend the Kori Rotti (chicken and flat bread) amongst the many veg and non-veg options. Pulimunchi (banana leaf wrap) is another favourite.

2. SHETTY LUNCH HOME, KUNDAPUR
Ghee Roast — two words that represent the best-loved dish of Kundapur. Shetty Lunch Home is the self-professed founding father of the dish, but no one is complaining as they do dish out the best version one could ever have. The delicious Chicken Ghee Roast and Kane (fish) Fry are the other highlights that have both tourists and locals thronging the restaurant.

3. HOTEL KWALITY, BHATKAL
Good enough to upstage any biryani in the world, Hotel Kwality is known for its *navayath* (newcomers) style Bhatkali Biryani. The origin of this style of biryani can be traced back to Arab traders, possibly getting the moniker of 'navyaths' from that era. The biryani is cooked with chunks of mutton or meat of your choice, with onions and spices and then rice is added later. The combination is then further cooked in a ceramic pot, making the flavours seep every grain of rice.

4. DIANA, UDIPI
If you're up for gastronomic adventures, then visit Diana in Udipi for its famous Gadbad (trouble) Ice Cream. A household name in the religious city of Udipi, this is a great pit stop for both north Indian and south Indian food, but only to be topped up with the iconic dessert.

5. HOTEL AMRUT, KARWAR
A family-run restaurant, Hotel Amrut dishes out the best Rava Fry Fish and Ghee Roast. This is not a place to be calorie conscious as large dollops of *ghee* and oil plop on frying pans to make the dishes taste as delicious as they do.

1. **DHARWAD**
   Tumbu Gai (aubergines stuffed with ground peanut and sesame, along with a number of spices)

2. **DAVANGERE**
   Benne Dosa (butter dosa) and Guladiki Unndi (sweet)

3. **BENGALURU**
   Ragi Mudde (ragi balls) with Kosambari (salad made from pulses and mustard seeds)

4. **MYSURU**
   Mysore Pak (rich sweet with copious amounts of *ghee*

5. **MADDUR**
   Vada (savoury fritter)

6. **UDIPI**
   Masala Dosa

7. **MANGALURU (SOUTH MALNAD)**
   Kori Rotti (dry rice flakes dipped in gravy), Bangude Pulimunchi (spicy sour mackerels) and Neer Dosa (lacy rice-crêpes)

8. **KODAGU**
   Pandi (pork) Curry with a hint of tanginess infused by kokum kachampuli (tart vinegar)

9. **SAKLESHPUR**
   Chattituttu (mixture of ground rice with spices and onions made crisp on the frying pan) and Kaalu Kadabu (rice dumplings)

HAVYAKA CUISINE

'Havyaka' is the name given to Dravida Brahmins who follow the Advaita philosophy, introduced by Adi Shankaracharya. The sect is lacto vegetarian in diet, making their cuisine simple yet delicious. Some unique dishes include *tellavu* (dosa), *todedev* (paper-thin sweet), *holige* (sweet), *thambli* (buttermilk), *hagalkai hashi* (bittergourd guard salad) and various chutneys. Bamboo shoot is an important ingredient for this region.

Havyaka cuisine is based on the natural leafy ingredients of the region, including leaves, roots, herbs and barks of trees; this can be traced back to the fact that many Brahmins lived in villages tucked away in forests, which were rich in these ingredients.

ABOUT *the* AUTHOR

Supriya has over a decade's experience in design and development of travel content for television, digital and print platforms. This includes writing and editing articles for national & international publications, curating a column, developing content for coffee-table books to writing scripts for TV shows and spearheading projects in the digital marketing space. Of her many travel writing *avatars*, she is happiest on the road when penning a guidebook – it has something to do with the comprehensiveness of knowing a destination and the thrill of being on the road for long stretches. She has authored/co-authored over 30 books on travel and plans to stop only when she hits a 100. Find out more on www.supriyasehgal.com.

INDEX

A

Aati Kalanja 41
Abbey Falls 155
Achyutaraya Temple 200
Agastya Lake 188, 189
Agumbe 129
Aihole 30, 185, 192
Anegudde Sri Vinayaka Temple 124
Anegundi 197, 200
Anshi Dandeli Tiger Reserve 179, 181
Asar Mahal 210

B

Baba Budangiri 163, 164
Badami 30, 185-190
Bahamani Fort, Tombs 211, 212
Baindur Beach 28, 126
Bandipur 28, 145-150
Banerghatta National Park 56
Basavakalyan 31, 207, 211
Belur 25, 99, 101, 103-107, 161, 171
Bengaluru 15, 21-25, 50-76, 80-83, 85, 99
Benne Dosa 40, 175, 177
Bhadra Tiger Reserve 171
Bharachukki Falls 78
Bheemeshwari 16, 48, 76
Bhutanatha Temples 189
Bhutha Kola 42, 130
Bidar 31, 207, 209, 211, 215
Birdwatching 76, 80, 149, 158, 168, 171
Bisle Reserve Forest 108
Brahmagiri Trek 154, 157
Brindavan Gardens 86, 90
Bylakuppe 147, 155

C

Camping 16, 148, 150, 157, 165
Canoeing 148, 156, 157
Carnatic music 41
Cauvery River 78-79, 82-83, 154-156
Cauvery Wildlife Sanctuary 79
Cave Temples 187, 194
Chamunda Devi 19
Chamundeshwari Temple 86, 90, 94
Chamundi Hill 85
Chand Bawdi 210
Chandragiri 26, 107
Chandramouleshwara Temple 179
Chandravalli Caves 81, 177
Channapatna 22
Chaturmukha Basadi 118, 135
Chikmagalur 29, 161-171
Chitradurga 81-82, 173, 175, 177
Coffee Museum 166
Coin Museum 27, 124
Coracle ride 76, 201
Cubbon Park 56, 57

D

Dandeli 30, 173, 175, 176, 179-183
Daroji Sloth Bear Sanctuary 197, 201
Davangere 40, 173-177, 220
Devaraja Market 93
Devbagh Beach 142, 143
Dharamsthala 19, 216
Dharwad 30, 173, 175, 179, 220
Dodda Alada Mara 22
Dodda Basavanagudi 57
Dollu Kunitha 43
Dubare Elephant Camp 154, 155

F

Ferozabad Fort 211

G

Gagan Mahal 211
Galibore 79, 80
Ganesh Habba 39
Gerusoppa 135
Ghathargi Bhagayavanti Temple 211
Ghee Roast 219
Goddess Chamundeshwari 38, 96
Gokarna 26, 111-114, 137-141, 217
Gol Gumbaz 209
Gorur Dam 104

Government Museum 59, 117, 211
Gudavi Bird Sanctuary 135
Guru Basadi 118

H

HAL Heritage Centre and Aerospace Museum 60
Halebeedu 25, 80, 99, 101, 104, 107, 171
Hampi 30, 39, 185, 197-204
Hassan 25, 29, 99, 101-108, 161, 171
Havyaka Cuisine 220
Hebbe Falls 165, 166
Hessarghatta 74, 77
Hikes 145, 148, 152, 157, 165, 171
Honnemaradu 176, 177
Horanadu 163, 166, 167
Hoysala 25, 80, 81, 98-104, 167, 170
Hubli 30, 173-179
Hyder Ali 36, 52, 56, 59, 81, 86, 177

I

Ibrahim Rouza 209
Ikkeri 133, 134
Indira Gandhi Glass House Garden 179
Innovative Film City 23
INTACH 53, 194
Iruppu Falls 154
ISKCON Temple 55

J

Jaggahalige Kunitha 43
Jami Masjid 211
Jawaharlal Nehru Planetarium 61
Jog Falls 26, 111, 131, 132, 176
Jomlu Theertha Falls 125
Jungle Safari 148
Jyothi Raj 81, 177

K

Kabini 28, 145-153
Kalaburagi 211
Kalasi 133
Kali Tiger Reserve 181
Kambala 130
Kamsale 43
Karadimajal 47
Karangolu 44

Karez system 214
Karwar 26, 111, 142, 143, 219
Kavala Caves 181
Kayaking 76, 79, 80, 148, 156, 157, 171
Keladi Museum 133
Keladi Temple 133
Kemmanagundi 163-166
Kempe Gowda 51, 52, 56, 58
Kodachadri Peak 176
Kodagu 28, 145-148, 154-159, 220
Kodava Hockey Festival 158
Kokkare Bellur 24
Kombat 44
KSRTC 37, 47, 48, 111, 185, 196
Kudle Beach 137, 138, 139, 140, 141
Kudremukh 163, 167, 170
Kudroli Gokarnanatheshwara 116, 119
Kudubi Holi 45

L

Lal Bagh Botanical Gardens 56
Lepakshi 74, 76
Lighthouse Island 142
Lord Gomateshwara 26, 107
Lotus Mahal & Elephant Stables 200

M

Maddur 24, 80
Madikeri 155, 157
Mahabaleshwar Temple 137, 138
Mahishasura 38, 91
Malik-E-Maidan 209
Mallikarjuna Temple 133, 163, 191, 192
Mangaluru 26, 111-122, 130, 157, 220
Manjarabad Fort 108
Masinagudi 147, 150, 152
Micro Light Flying 148, 156
Mirjan Fort 139
Mookambika 19, 124, 176, 216
Mudumalai 147, 152
Mullayangiri 163-165
Muppane 132
Murudeshwar 113, 123-126
Mysore Dusshera 38, 85, 94
Mysore Palace 38, 86, 89, 91, 95, 96
Mysuru 21, 84-86, 89-97, 220

Experience Karnataka

N

Nagarhole National Park 147, 152
Namdroling Monastery 29, 155
Nandi Hills 75
NGMA 54
Nilgiri Biosphere 17, 46, 145
Nisargadhama 48, 114, 119, 155
NITK lighthouse 27, 122
Nrityagram Dance School 77
Nrupatunga Hill 175, 179

O

Om Beach 137, 138, 140, 141
Omkareshwara Temple 155
One Tree Point 137

P

Panambur 27, 122
Pandi Curry 40, 159
Papanatha Temple 191
Pattadakal 30, 185-191
Pilikula Nisargadhama 48, 114

Q

Quad biking 148, 157
Queen's Bath 198, 199

R

Rafting 80, 148, 154-156, 167, 180
Ramnagar 23
Ranganathittu Bird Sanctuary 82
Rangeen Mahal 213
Rava Fry Fish 219
Ravana Phadi Cave Temples 194
River Tern Lodge 171
Rosario Cathedral 116
Royal Mysore Walks 94

S

Sakleshpur 25, 99, 101, 107, 108, 109, 220
Sakrebailu Elephant Camp 176
Sandur 187, 204, 205
Shettihalli Church 102
Shimoga 30, 173-178
Shivanasamudra Waterfalls 78
Shravanabelagola 25, 99, 101, 106
Somanathapura 80, 101, 171
Sri Krishna Math 114, 122, 217

Sri Manjunatha Swamy Temple 216
Sri Mookambika Devi 216
Sri Samsthana Mahabaleshwara Deva 217
Sri Sharada Peetham 131, 216
St Aloysius Chapel 116
St Mary's Basilica 60
St Mary's Island 126
St Philomena's Church 89
Suggi Kunitha 44
Surathkal 122, 219
Syntheri Rocks 179

T

Tadiandamol Trek 157
Takht Mahal 213
Tala Kaveri 155
Talakkad 83
Tannir Bavi Beach 27, 122
Tarkash Mahal 214
Tipu Sultan 36, 52, 86, 108, 187, 188
Trekking 76, 79, 148, 163, 165, 168, 170
Tungabhadra River 187, 198, 200

U

Udipi 26, 111, 121-125, 129, 153, 217, 219
Ugaadi 39, 43, 99
Ulavi Channabasaveshwar Temple 180
Ulsoor Lake 52, 72
Unkal Lake 175, 179
Upli Burj 209
Urwa Marigudi 115

V

Vajra Waterfall 182
Veerabhadraswamy Temple 76, 83
Venkataramana Temple 115, 119, 141
Vijayapura 31, 207-211
Vikarama Shetty Basadi 118
Virupaksha Temple 188, 197-199, 203, 204
Virupapur Gaddi 197, 198, 202, 203

W

Wodeyar 36, 82, 83, 86, 91, 95
Wonder La 22, 61

Y

Yakshagana 42, 43, 130
Yana Rocks 139